Reflecting on Faith
in a Post-Christian Time

THE LIVING ISSUES DISCUSSION SERIES

*T*HE LIVING ISSUES DISCUSSION SERIES IS EDITED by Michael A. King and published by Cascadia Publishing House (earlier Pandora Press U.S.) as well as sometimes copublished with Herald Press. Cascadia Publishing House, in consultation with its Editorial Council as well as volume editors and authors, is primarily responsible for content of these studies, which—typically through main text by author and a chapter of affirming and critical evaluations by respondents—address "living issues" likely to benefit from lively and serious discussion.

Reflecting on Faith
in a Post-Christian Time

Daniel Liechty

Foreword by Duane Friesen

<u>Living Issues Discussion Series, Volume 3</u>

Cascadia

Publishing House
the new name of Pandora Press U.S.
Telford, Pennsylvania

copublished with
Herald Press
Scottdale, Pennsylvania

Cascadia Publishing House orders, information, reprint permissions:
contact@CascadiaPublishingHouse.com
1-215-723-9125
126 Klingerman Road, Telford PA 18969
www.CascadiaPublishingHouse.com

Reflecting on Faith in a Post-Christian Time
First edition published 1990 by SCM Press and
Trinity Press International, as *Theology in Postliberal Perspective*
This edition copyright © 2003 by
Cascadia Publishing House, Telford, PA 18969
(formerly Pandora Press U.S.)
All rights reserved
Copublished with Herald Press, Scottdale, PA
Library of Congress Catalog Number: 2002041007
ISBN: 1-931038-12-0
Printed in Canada by Pandora Press
Book design by Cascadia Publishing House
Cover design by Jonathan Peachey

The paper used in this publication is recycled and meets the
minimum requirements of American National Standard for Information Sciences—Permanence of Paper for Printed Library Materials, ANSI Z39.48-
1984.1984

All Bible quotations are used by permission, all rights reserved, and are from
the *New Revised Standard Version Bible*, copyright 1989, by the Division of Christian Education of the National Council of the Churches of Christ in the USA.

Library of Congress Cataloguing-in-Publication Data
Liechty, Daniel, 1954-
    Reflecting on faith in a post-Christian time / Daniel Liechty.
        p. cm. -- (Living issues discussion series ; v. 3)
    Rev. ed. of: Theology in postliberal perspective. 1990.
    Includes bibliographical references (p.) and index.
    ISBN 1-931038-12-0 (alk. paper)
        1. Theology, Doctrinal. 2. Postliberal theology. 3. Mennonites--
Doctrines. I. Liechty, Daniel, 1954- Theology in postliberal perspec-
tive. II. Title. III. Living issues discussion series ; 3.

BT83.8 .L54 2003
230'.97--dc21

                                                                    2002041007

        12 11 10 09 08 07 06 05 04 03   10 9 8 7 6 5 4 3 2

CONTENTS

THE FOREWORD

Who are we humans and how do we respond to our mortality? Drawing on Ernst Becker's "theory of generative morality anxiety" Daniel Liechty proposes that "taming this terror is quite literally the most important human task" (p. 35). We can choose the path of acceptance by taking responsibility to nurture an inclusive freedom of the human soul and spirit. Or we can deny death by devoting our lives to the illusory pursuit of projects to preserve our immortality. Flight from mortality is the root of evil, resulting in projects that repress the human spirit through authoritarian dogma, domination and violence. We see a contemporary demonstration of Liechty's thesis in the United States pursuit of imperial domination of the world through military might. The refusal to accept our human limits is manifest in the effort to eradicate evil, which paradoxically perpetuates even more evil.

Liechty persuasively delineates the explanatory power of Becker's paradigm. The question raised for me is whether that paradigm is a universal explanation for the human predicament. Does the theory account as well for those who are poor, without power, and experience life on the underside, who do not have the option to pursue projects to preserve immortality?

He claims as his method religious reflection, not theology, though the book addresses central theological concerns such as our models of God, the roots of evil, and Christology. I welcome Liechty's provocative thinking, some of which is sure to raise eyebrows. Being married to a Jewish wife, keeping a Jewish household, and his professional experience as a clinical social worker inform his creative challenge to traditional Christian belief and practice. I hope the church is ready to welcome him as a conversation partner. We need more provocative proposals like Liechty's to awaken us from our dogmatic slumbers.

Liechty's religious reflection is, above all, grounded in a real human Jesus whose orientation is theocentric, not focused on himself. He suggests that the church needs to move beyond dogma to rediscover a Jesus who models the way of acceptance of mortality in his teachings and life of nonviolence. He supports the uniqueness and universal relevance of Jesus but criticizes those who hold to the superiority and exclusiveness of Christian truth.

Though Liechty views Jesus as the "paradigmatic incarnation of God's spirit in history," he advocates that the church become more open and accepting of a wide spectrum opinions in relation to the doctrine of the Trinity. The Trinity compromises the Oneness of God, and is simply unnecessary baggage from the tradition that is no longer functional for healing, ethical responsibility, and dialogue with persons of other monotheistic faiths. Liechty's controlling principle is a "functional social and political hermeneutic." He reminds us that Anabaptists held to a diversity of points of view on this dogma. He criticizes a number of contemporary Mennonite theologians who make the Trinity central to their thought. His ideas are sure to provoke further conversation among Mennonite theologians.

In view of Liechty's own functional hermeneutic, could not one make a persuasive rendering of trinitarian thought that serves the very path of acceptance that leads to healing and renewal of the human spirit for which Liechty yearns? Is that not what Gordon Kaufman (a theologian to whom Liechty is deeply indebted) does in his major work, *In Face of Mystery*?

In a provocative appendix on September 11, Liechty rightly challenges pacifists to think through, more carefully than we have, that we do benefit from defense and protection, and we do desire protection and defense from harm. Liechty answers his own challenge with a form of vocational pacifism. Though we do benefit from protection, pacifist Christians should not participate in violence in the defense of the nation, lest we be "salt without savor." In a democratic and pluralistic society there is a need for people with an alternative vision that transcends national self-interest and narrow patriotic loyalties.

In our "post-Christian" world of radical pluralism, Liechty is committed to a free church perspective. He believes it is less bound to the authoritarian structures of institutional religion. It is thus ideally suited to respond to the deep spiritual needs of people. This vision of life will nurture a spirituality that involves an immediacy of relationship with God, an ethic of discipleship oriented to following the example of Jesus, and a commitment to the church as a disciplined community where relationships of mutual love and care are nurtured and sustained.

—*Duane Friesen, North Newton, Kansas*
  Professor of Bible and Religion, Bethel College

SERIES EDITOR'S PREFACE

*B*ecause Daniel Liechty's topic, "reflecting on faith in a post-Christian time" is a "living issue" that deserves serious discussion and an examination of various ways Christians understand such agenda, Liechty's book fits the Living Issues Discussion Series. To set the conversation in motion, typically books in the series include a vigorous statement of position regarding an issue or set of issues sometimes controversial in faith circles. Then, after a book's main text, a Responses chapter provides affirming and critical commentary followed by discussion resources.

The result in this case is a fascinating blend. First, as the core of the book, Liechty testifies to his understanding of which elements of Christianity are likely to do more harm than good in a post-Christian time, and which still contribute to a meaningful faith rooted in and shaping what is so needed in our era—nonviolent thinking and living.

Then four respondents, Christian Early, Marlin Jeschke, Michele Hershberger, and Brian McLaren, ponder carefully and often with passion to rival Liechty's how Liechty's convictions fit—or not—their understanding of Christian faith. Each assesses what elements such faith requires if it is to remain linked to historic Christian affirmations and sufficiently robust to meet the challenges of our era. Each sees merit in Liechty's proposals and each also, particularly the first three, raises concerns.

Perhaps especially in light of the intensity of some of the challenges the respondents pose, it should be emphasized that they were specifically invited to go beyond the glowing-affirmations-only evaluations which tend to ensue when publishers request advance comment on books. Rather, they were to feel free to articulate both affirmation *and* criticism of Liechty's views. The result, from my point of view as series editor, was precisely what was hoped for: a variety of insightful interactions with Liechty that set in motion already within the pages of *Reflecting on Faith in a Post-Christian Era* a dynamic dialogue.

Within this dialogue I spy particularly three questions. The first involves when in efforts to link Christianity with thought forms of the day the latter absorb the former. Many respondents see this as key and worry especially that once Liechty reconceptualizes the divine there is not enough left of a God who is, to put it simply, really there. This is an important worry and one it seems to me, a pastor who most Sundays would not find Liechty's God quite "real" enough to preach, for Liechty to address.

But there is also the question of how Christians should balance commitment to inhouse assumptions with readiness to communicate in ways accessible to those not in the "house." When I wrote a dissertation within a rhetoric program in a secular university, I aimed to ponder what could be learned by viewing the church more from outside than inside, without giving the church the only say in setting terms of the discussion (such as maybe by claiming insight through special biblical revelation which I do affirm as a preacher but which was unlikely within my university setting to be seen as carrying the day). Liechty seems to work at a similar project in this book. As McLaren more enthusiastically affirms, but other respondents also acknowledge if with more unease, this grants Liechty entrée into circles of thought where the riches of his faith might otherwise be dismissed. That is a significant contribution and might even, if I dare here draw back in the language of my "churchly" commitments as pastor, be considered an aspect of Liechty's ministry. Something like this is what McLaren eloquently celebrates in connecting Liechty's concerns with those of persons on the verge of losing faith.

Finally there is the question of how differences in perspective should be managed. Should birds of Liechty's feather flock together and those oriented to operating largely within historic Christian convictions remain happily in their own flock, neither flock challenging or learning from the other? I hope not. I hope this book helps flocks of more than one feather do more thinking together than they often do and even inspires them to do some flying together in an era when, God (however conceived) knows, we too often thud separately to the ground.

—*Michael A. King, Living Issues Discussion Series Editor*

AUTHOR'S PREFACE: CONTINUITY AND REVISION

*I*t has been over fifteen years since I wrote the first version of this book.[1] These years have seen a good number of significant changes in my life. On the personal side, I married a person of a religious background different from my Mennonite one. My wife is Jewish and we keep a (modern) Jewish household. I also became a father for the first time, which has given me a sense of personal investment in the future I didn't even know I lacked before the blessed event. Professionally, I left religious studies and retrained in clinical social work. I was affiliated for a number of years as a group specialist in an in-patient, psychiatric institution, then for some five years more in a hospice setting, where I practiced individual and family therapy with dying people. Most recently, I have been teaching clinical social work on the graduate level. When I wrote the first version of this material, my intention was to address the professional lay audience, educated in fields other than theology. I write now as one fully part of that audience.

It is a distinctly fortuitous opportunity to take a mid-career look at what was written fifteen years earlier, to see what has held up well and where my mind has changed. I find that the basic approach has held up well. It has allowed me to move with my most deeply held values and convictions into contact with people of quite different beliefs, there to seek understanding and to interact therapeutically, even on occasion pastorally, all the while maintaining a mutual respect for their beliefs and mine. The changes I notice in making these revisions are mainly those of emphasis rooted in further experience.

13

In the original introduction, I situated this volume in conversation with philosophical deconstruction. I suggested that the American religious tradition imbibed deeply at the well of pluralism and pragmaticism almost from its inception, and that deconstruction was therefore hardly the scandal on the American religious scene it had been in some other areas of learning. I say with some confidence that deconstruction is now more or less forgotten, and we are free to resituate this revision into different conversations.

I initially chose to characterize my reflections as "postliberal." My use of this term can best be understood in relation to the classical Protestant liberal theology of the nineteenth century. Although in my college and seminary training I had been taught quite pointedly the many errors of classical liberal theology, I subsequently came to deeply appreciate at least one of its central interpretive theological principles—that the proper study for human beings is the human being. That is, when we human beings think about our spiritual experiences, giving voice to that aspect of our individual and communal life in the language and rituals of religion, that language and those rituals themselves become the proper object of further reflection, telling us mainly about the ways in which we human beings navigate and make sense of our world.

The enduring, legitimate criticism of classical liberal theology had little to do with this interpretive principle. Indeed, a number of liberal theology's central projects, for example, the concern to sort out the human Jesus of Nazareth from the magisterial Christ of Christian theology, although shelved for a generation or two, have returned to occupy a primary place in current spiritual quests. We are again being invited to meet the historical Jesus for the first time.[2] This clearly indicates that although classical liberal theology had many problems, it also touched on very pivotal and long-term human spiritual concerns that cannot be ignored.

This realization alone should cause us to reconsider liberal religious thought in a more positive light. Karl Barth and others turned away from liberal theology because of the First World War. They rightly were scandalized to see their own professors and teachers line up behind their respective nationalisms, offering their religious blessing to the soldiers of both sides marching off into the first of many major, prolonged killing frenzies that came to characterize the recently passed century. Their criticism is valid and is part of the heritage passed on to subsequent generations. But those of us trying to make sense of life spiritually as we move now into the twenty-first century have seen that the neo-ortho-dox approach of Barth and others also had clay feet. We watched a good many of our American *Neo* professors and teachers as they blessed the soldiers marching off to the Second World War, Viet-nam, the Persian Gulf. We watched as they constructed theologi-cal justifications for American and NATO nuclear weapons poli-cies, in general playing their horns in the Cold War band, cheer-leading for American Capitalism against the socialist Evil Em-pire, or asserting the national right to Middle Eastern oil reserves.

Yet while the reflections I offer here have definite affinities with the classical liberal religious style, it will also be clear that these reflections are formulated on this side of (especially) Rein-hold Niebuhr's criticism of liberal individualism, its optimism about human nature, its faith in the innate moral goodness of people, and in the inevitability of progress in human history. To the extent that nineteenth-century liberalism is associated with modernist style of consciousness, therefore, the reflections I offer are definitely postmodern. I am uneasy with the label *postmod-ern*, however. Its meaning is extremely liquid and it has become something of a fad term. To the extent that postmodernism de-scribes a style of consciousness, my sense is that we are only be-ginning to see this consciousness developing and have little idea of what is really occuring.[3]

I remain satisfied, overall, with the term *postliberal* to describe my approach. Postliberal contains echoes of the anthropological starting point taken over from classical liberal theology. At the same time, it reminds us that we are moving beyond that liberal-ism, incorporating the enduring aspects of Niebuhr's criticism of liberal optimism about the goodness of human nature and the in-evitability of cumulative, beneficial progress in human history. Postliberal as I used it was modeled after John Macquarrie's use of the term and was a conscious attempt to invite parallels espe-cially with Reinhold and Richard Niebuhr's views, most particu-larly with Reinhold Niebuhr's view of the human condition.[4] As a former student of John Howard Yoder, I experienced the Niebuhr brothers as sort of the bogeymen in my ethics training. I have been in the process of critically reappropriating the views of the Niebuhrs since my seminary days. Now that I have come to be living right in the same physical location in which the brothers were raised, the ongoing conversation is more intimate than ever.

During the past decade or so, however, the term postliberal has come to be used almost exclusively to designate the cultural-linguistic theory of doctrine offered by George Lindbeck.[5] While some echoes of agreement with Lindbeck's ideas are present in my reflections, I clearly had the Niebuhrs and not Lindbeck in mind in my use of the term. On the whole, I agree with Gordon Kaufman's evaluation of Lindbeck's work, that there are implications in the cultural-linguistic approach for progressively critical religious reflection that Lindbeck does not explore.[6] Hopefully, I have at least begun to explore some of these implications in this work. In deference to the current use of postliberal to designate the approach of Lindbeck and his students, I relinquish it for the purposes of this revised edition of my book.

The *interfaith* perspective was present in my original work, but my sense that it is of absolutely central importance for responsible religious reflection has grown more strongly during recent years. The unavoidable cultural context for all religious reflection, in America to be sure, but also now globally (and with increasing urgency after 9-11-01), is the very real situation of thorough religious pluralism.

This situation of extreme pluralism, in which ideas increasingly compete for acceptance and validation in a free market, can be disorienting and even threatening to traditional religious belief. Much traditional belief tells us that there is but one truth in life, and strongly implies or teaches overtly that those who do not hold that truth should not be experiencing love, joy, meaning, happiness, fulfillment, and confidence of connection with divine transcendence in their lives, at least certainly not in equal measure as those who do know and believe the one truth. Yet all of us have come to see that this expectation is clearly not true. Evidence points to the premise that many paths, both spiritual and secular, yield living fruits of love, joy, meaning, happiness, fulfillment and a sense of divine connection. Likewise, persons following many paths appear to experience personal, family, and social dysfunction (the fruits of sin) in about equal measure.

These easily verifiable observations must give any thinking people pause before they plunge ahead insisting on the universal and exclusionary absoluteness of the Truth of their own particular spiritual path. Perhaps it is my American pragmatism that places these observations front and center in my spiritual reflections. Pragmatism suggests that human thoughts and actions are motivated by the tension created between our needs (in the broadest sense—including physical, mental, psychological, and spiritual aspects of our being) and the environment that must satisfy those needs. We think and act to reduce this tension.

In this case, there is a clear tension in what we observe and what our traditional culturally fashioned religious beliefs predict should be the differences between those who know and believe the one Truth and those who do not. This tension spurs us to thought and action. In the case of the many varieties of fundamentalism, this tension spurs thought and action in the direction of hunkering down all the more tightly to the received tradition, either by refusing to see what is now clearly in front of our eyes in the lives of our neighbors, friends, work associates, fellow PTA members, or by turning up the volume on apologetic special pleading that compares the best examples of one's own tradition with the worst examples of other traditions.

This fundamentalism is, at best, a holding pattern. It does not create forward movement for our tradition or for the human project. As a parent, I have been working hard to instill in my toddler the simple notion of the Golden Rule, one of the most basic axioms of civilized communitarian living. Do to others the same thing you want them to do you. If you expect something from others, then they have the right to expect the same from you, and you have the obligation to return to others anything that you have asked of them for yourself.

Unless I am ready to insist that my spiritual path is exempt from this basic rule of civilized, communal living (and I am not), then this pattern, in light of observations above, sets the parameters for an interfaith approach to spiritual reflection. That which I expect for myself as I attempt to communicate what I have found—respect for my Truth, willingness to listen with ears that are open, sympathetic consideration of the best of my tradition rather than only looking for the worst of it, generosity of spirit and tolerance for the human foibles that creep in and tarnish our message, I must be willing to give in full measure to others.[7]

In this cultural context, interfaith religious reflection can never assume a position other than that of dialogue on all matters with which it concerns itself. The evangelical position that biblical faith is somehow qualitatively different from and superior to all other religions (as I was taught in my denominational seminary) lacks this basic generosity of spirit.[8]

I have come to see more powerfully than ever that writing of a religiously reflective nature must be judged not only by the clarity with which it communicates material within its own tradition, but also by the generous respect and charitable attitude of dialogue with which one can approach the teachings of other traditions from within the frame of reference being offered. The best approaches will not only have allowances for (optional) dialogue with other traditions. They will actively encourage reaching out for such dialogue. That is a central guiding principle in what I present here, in both the affirmative ideas and in the tentative criticism I offer of aspects of my own tradition. At the same time, as I hope will become clear, I do not accept the completely relativistic conception that all religions are equal, the same, without qualitative distinctions that can and should be applied to evaluate and criticize the manifestations of religion in specific contexts.

Special notice should be made at this point of another guiding principle in my reflection. We do have a general obligation to allow the truth of other faith traditions to function critically for us. But as Christians, living in the wake of 2000 years of Christian history, we have a specific mandate, duty, and requirement to root out and finally erase the poisonous remnants of Christian anti-Judaism that continue to linger in our teachings about God, Christ, redemption and salvation. As James Carroll (to cite only one recent writer on this subject among many others) copiously documented in his book, *Constantine's Sword—The Church and the Jews*, this tradition of anti-Judaism extends back to the earliest years of the Christian era and by now is deeply entangled in nearly every aspect of Christian Scripture, belief, and doctrine.[9]

It will undoubtedly take many generations of consciously informed will to remove this deforming toxin completely from Christian teaching and ideology. It has been a guiding principle in what I present here to have done the best I possibly could not to pass on in any way this tradition of Christian anti-Judaism.[10] If I had not done at least this much, then it would have been better had this book not been written at all. The same should be said of any other creative work of contemporary Christian thought.

I specifically characterize this writing as religious *reflection*. This is an intended communication of what the book contains.

As I mentioned above, I left the field of religious studies to retrain in clinical social work. I no longer consider myself a specialist in theology. Whatever theological reading I can squeeze in here and there is very unsystematic, guided much more by whatever happens to catch my interest than by an attempt to keep up and stay abreast of currently breaking material in the field.

I remember in my seminary days how annoyed I got at the students training for congregational ministry who would inquire sharply and early in any investigation of some theological question, "Is this of any use in the pulpit?" In other words, what is the concrete, practical value of placing so much intellectual energy into this question? At the time, I saw this as inexcusably antiintellectual. Now, at this juncture in my life, although I ask a somewhat different question (my question is directed toward the concrete value an argument or concept has in helping people sort through the existential issues of meaning and purpose in daily living), I must admit I have joined camp with the ministers-intraining. I quickly tire of theological discourse that seems removed from concrete living, smacks of arcane intellectualism, and is directed only at other specialized scholars.

I might say that this is one more example in my life illustrating the Jungian observation that we tend to acquire exactly those characteristics and traits in later life that especially annoyed us in others when we were young. Ironically, some of those congregational ministers-in-training have by now become academic theologians and continue to annoy me, now from the other side!

One of my intended points of communication, therefore, in choosing to characterize this material as a reflection is to signal that it is not a work of specialized, academic theology, neither in method nor in content. I make no claim to be current on any front in theological studies and fully accept in advance the criticisms of theological specialists who will be offended that I exhibit no acquaintance with this or that writer or line of argument.

On the other hand, I do hope that the use of this term indicates that I intend to offer serious, disciplined reflection. As an educated nonspecialist, I do think about what I believe, about my living faith, and seek to make this faith comprehensible to myself and to others. My goal in this volume is not to exhibit my skill at touching all the theological bases, but rather to invite the reader to reflect upon, to think about, the ways the conceptions of our religious faith are shaped by some of the sociocultural, historical, psychological, and spiritual forces present in our society, and to step back from these influences long enough to get some handle on understanding the specific forms these beliefs take within our specific individual and collective context. If I am even remotely successful in this, I think the value of the book will speak for itself, despite its obvious vulnerabilities to the criticisms of theological specialists.

Although it is not in my title, I also want to explicitly place my reflection in the context of a growing movement of "progressive Protestantism." The progressive Protestant perspective is more difficult to define exactly, but it might be possible to outline a few basic principles that communicate a general idea of what I have in mind. A book by Robert McAfee Brown,[11] *The Spirit of Protestantism*, comes to mind when I think about what I mean by a progressive Protestant perspective. Brown presented Protestantism as a positive concept rather than primarily a protest against, and specifically endorsed theologian Paul Tillich's notion of the "Protestant Principle." Aware of the human propensity for rendering absolute loyalty to partial realities (in short, idolatry), the Protestant Principle designates a determination to always move beyond such loyalties whenever and wherever they are recognized, even when these claims to absolute loyalty are made in the name of the church itself. One of the principles of progressive Protestantism is a keen recognition that such claims are regularly made and encouraged in the name of religion, including the Christian religion.

As one of Mennonite background, I see in the sixteenth-century representatives of the so-called "Radical Reformation," as well as in seventeenth-century Quakers and others, a clear expression of this Protestant Principle. I am proud to place my general views in direct historical line with this Radical Reformation tradition.

One of the enduring beliefs I gained from my Mennonite upbringing is a thoroughgoing commitment to an ethic of pacifism. My own struggle with the question of authority, in religion, morals, ethics, and psychological and spiritual life in general, began in earnest as I determined to work through a consistently pacifist approach to religious understanding. Pacifism here is shorthand for an embracing a commitment to live peaceably in the broadest sense—living peaceably with fellow human beings, other species, and with the environment. It is a style of living that does not assume conflict between self and others inevitably includes violence, and therefore does not prepare for violent conflict in advance (especially by arming oneself). If violence should occur, primary energy is then directed toward reconciliation rather than revenge.

My continuing goal is to construct a frame of reference for spiritual understanding in which commitment to pacifism is fundamentally integrated into the frame of reference itself, not simply one option among others for an isolated ethics tacked onto the end, long after the real spiritual drama has already occurred elsewhere. While I do not claim to have fully succeeded in this goal, I am pleased to offer these reflections as an interim account of where I am heading.[12]

I have come to see that pacifism is finally anarchistic in relation to questions of authority. Authority is decisively a question of power. Pacifism is by nature skeptical of power. In an earlier attempt to present an anarchistic theology,[13] while I think I was successful in formulating a theology of anarchism, I was ultimately unsatisfied with the results because I was appealing to a specific, biblical source of external and transcendental authority for what I was writing.[14]

The question of authority is with me at every point in these pages. Although I have by no means solved this problem of authority for religious reflection, I have become increasingly confident of the idea that authority must reside with the author. Religious reflection is similar to the writing of a poet or novelist, in that it employs words creatively, constructing a mental picture that invites others to experience their world in new ways. The author hopes readers will find in this new perspective something of value for their daily living. A measure of success in such a piece of writing is whether, in fact, readers find in their appropriation of the text new ways of perceiving their world of experience.

One final point should be made explicit. While the synthetic work of social anthropologist Ernest Becker is certainly present in the earlier version of this book, during the intervening years I have engaged in a much more in-depth study of Becker's work[15] and for the past few years have been pursuing that study with people in a variety of fields across disciplinary boundaries.[16] I am confident that in his theory of generative death anxiety, Becker was onto something at the very heart of human motivation.[17] Becker himself died of cancer, in 1974 at age forty-nine, soon after he outlined the basic theory. During the past two decades, laboratory testing of the social psychological aspects of the theory of generative death anxiety, which now includes testing in at least four countries and across the age and socioeconomic spectra, has been showing the theory to be robust in predicting subject behavior in response to controlled stimuli.[18] That fact probably carries more weight with social scientists than with others, but it should indicate to any thinking person that this is a theory of human motivation worth serious respect and consideration.

In a (necessarily very succinct) nutshell, the theory of generative death anxiety suggests that self-consciousness and the ability to think abstractly (that is, to think of oneself in the third person) creates a very peculiar problem in human beings. Humans share with all successful species a strong instinct for survival. Yet human beings alone (as far as we can tell) are cognitively aware that death awaits each one of us. We are a species in which our key survival mechanism (our tremendously developed cerebral cortex, which helps abstract thinking and the creation of a personal sense of self) runs directly counter to one of the strongest and most pervasive instinctual urges possessed by all living beings—the urge to survive. This awareness of mortality potentially creates an all but overwhelming sense of anxiety with which each of us must live from a relatively early age. Were we continually conscious of our vulnerability and the real dangers this world presents, we would be stunned and unable to act in our environment.

Therefore, this anxiety must be repressed, and in this repression we have the beginnings of the distinctly human dynamic psychology. In short, the energy cooking away in the human subconscious is at root not simply sexual, aggressive, accumulative, mimetic, or acquisitive (to name only the best-known theoretical alternatives proposed by various schools of depth psychology). These are understood, rather, as particular, culturally formed manifestations of an even deeper generative death anxiety.

Most of the creative and forward-moving action we maintain in human existence is deeply motivated by the desire to deny human mortality and earn assurance of immortality by proving ourselves worthy. Likewise, as will be seen in chapter two, most of the evil human beings perpetrate on themselves individually, on their families and immediate others, in groups, as societies, and against the environment can be best understood as driven by obsessive pursuit of immortality projects (at various levels of abstraction) in ways compulsively blind to corrective evidential feedback. This is as clear a description of human sin as can be produced from within the analytic categories of social science.

In his final summation of his theoretical work,[19] Becker concluded that what he had been up to all along was a criticism of social science from the transcendent, ethical perspective most often associated with religion. He saw that his project was essentially the same as that of the great Protestant theologian, Paul Tillich. The difference was that Tillich was working from the side of religion-approaching-social-science, whereas Becker saw that he had been working from the side of social-science-approaching-religion.

This establishes, I believe, the appropriateness of placing Becker's theoretical work in such a central place of my religious reflections. My hope and expectation is that responses to these reflections, from critics and fellow travelers alike, will take the foundational theoretical work Becker provided into proper account.

—*Daniel Liechty*
  Normal, Illinois

Reflecting on Faith
in a Post-Christian Time

1

A STARTING POINT FOR RELIGIOUS REFLECTION

*A*s consciousness of self develops, we find ourselves on this earth, living out, give or take, our three-score-and-ten. It is a joy to be alive and for that we are happy. But life is not easy. Many of us have sicknesses and diseases. Many of us have deformities. There are real and genuine barriers between how we are living and how we would like to live. There is economic inequality, and the majority must work hard for a living while the few need not worry. There is oppression of the spirit and soul as well as of the body. There is injustice and fear. And in the end, death awaits. This is our situation; it is within it context that we strive to maintain the forward movement of life.

Immediately upon reflection, questions arise. Is this all there is to it? Can we say nothing in addition about the human condition? On what may we base our hopes? We can only begin with a hypothesis. Human beings are an evolved species on this earth engaged in an ongoing, puzzling and at times contradictory task of grasping and understanding the whole, of which we are only part. The main tool available for this is language. Human language is itself an artifact, a product of human community, whose origin and immediate function is itself still only dimly understood.

Human beings as a species are the result of a long and mixed evolutionary history we share with all past and present species. We are physical beings and share completely in nature's demand that a living species maintain adequate sources of nourishment, protection from the elements, and an environment in which to procreate in each generation.

If a living species cannot maintain these in each generation, the species dies. And species, even the mighty dinosaurs, have become extinct. Our earth is a generous mother. She provides us with all we need to flourish. Natural disasters do happen for various reasons and survival for most species has often been a hard struggle. In many ways human beings are more vulnerable than other animals. We are naked, weak, without instincts and in relation to an ability to survive independently are born premature. Despite this we have been a successful species. As we view the earth on which we live, it is possible and even compelling to give assent to the biblical assessment of the earth: And God saw that it was *good*.

Despite our relative physical vulnerability as a species, we have proven ourselves able to adapt to a wide variety of environmental conditions. We have been able to vary survival strategies and continue to live in altered environmental conditions where others of our animal siblings, with their mighty strength, speed, sharp claws, teeth and warm coats have failed. For human beings have the greatest advantage of all species in the struggle for survival. We have powers of observation and abstract reasoning as well as ability to learn new skills that exceed all of our animal siblings. We appropriate the natural gifts of our animal siblings. We cover ourselves with their warm coats and tough skins. We nourish ourselves on their muscles and milk. We make tools, weapons, and ornaments of their sharp teeth, claws, and strong bones. We have also mastered the laws governing plant life and can grow and store food for the future, making clothing of fiber and building shelter from wood and stone. We are indeed a very successful species, living and flourishing on a good earth.

We know that our mother the earth has not been kind to those species that could not adapt to changes in environmental conditions. Nor does the human species have unconditional hospitality promised on this earth. As a species we need not fear even the natural disasters—flood, drought, earthquakes—which are an ongoing part of the earth's working. These bring terrible tragedy to specific communities but do not affect species survival.

There is evidence, however, that abnormal disasters, such as a collision with large heavenly bodies, have occurred and have adversely affected the survival abilities of species now extinct.

Likewise, some scientists claim that certain such occurrences are inevitable—like the sun eventually burning out—which, at a distant point in the future will make our planet uninhabitable for life as we know it. We face life, therefore, with the full knowledge that not only is each individual human being mortal, but that the species itself will one day come to an end. Our mother the earth can no more promise us life forever than a human mother can promise that to her child. Nevertheless, we can affirm of our life on this earth that it is *good*.

Our mother the earth does provide us with all of the security and possibility to flourish we could desire. To demand more of her is nothing but ungrateful *hubris*. Yet we discuss the survival of the human race now in a manner more serious than in any previous generation. The end to our species would not be because of the inhospitality of the natural environment, but because of our own doing. In our quest to flourish on this earth, we have unlocked the secrets of the natural order that now, if we abuse this knowledge, could literally wipe us out in a short period of time. This is our own doing, for which we must take the full responsibility. The future of our race now rests in our own hands. We are no longer victims or passive agents. We are the first of species to become the architects of our future. Our physical evolutionary journey has brought us to this point and there can be no return to innocence.

* * *

We have been a successful species. On the other hand, we are relative newcomers here and the story of our success or failure is ours to finish. What will be the next chapter in the human story? Will we learn to contain the raging in our breast and create true community among ourselves and with the rest of our environment? Or will it finally be concluded that we are just one more of those curious species that have occurred during the evolutionary process, in line with the dinosaurs, a life-form in whom the very characteristics that allowed them for a time to adapt successfully in the end doomed them to extinction? This is the context out of which all serious probing of the human condition must be pursued.[1]

Caution must always be taken when asking questions about human nature. Human existence is rooted in the history of particular nations, races, cultures, and communities. What is assumed to be universal human nature in one context may be seen as nothing but outlandish behavior in another. (Just think of how easily we in our culture assume economic profit-seeking is simply human nature, whereas in many traditional societies this kind of behavior would appear as a transgression against the heavens.) The more we learn about human diversity, the more difficult it becomes to discern universals of human nature.

There are political grounds for caution as well. For the question of human nature occurs most often in challenging or justifying particular social, political, and economic relations. "Well, you can't change human nature now, can you?" Like appeals to special revelation from God, or more recently appeals to scientific fact,[2] the function of appeals to human nature is generally to cut off the discussion. It is an attempt to wield power, saying in effect, "Beyond this we cannot go!" Set notions of human nature, therefore, act as ideological blinders to new possibilities.

Yet we cannot avoid discussion of human nature altogether. Like all questions of ultimate concern, the question of human nature is perennial. The best we can do is to remain aware of the tendency to ideologize such probing. We cannot forget that central to our original hypothesis is that we stand *within* the whole we are trying to grasp and understand. Therefore, even as we move into a discussion of human nature, we must remain constantly aware that our conclusions are partial and tentative. None of us has a perch outside or above the human situation from which to decide what absolutely is true.

That kind of approach, characterized by Eric Voegelin as "gnosticism,"[3] has been rendered untenable by the awareness that all human thought proceeds from within particular social situations, reflecting a particular social situation and is a plea for particular political responses within that social situation. In discussion of universalizing concepts such as human nature, there must be a willingness to define and defend the political responses a particular position elicits. Universalizing concepts must not be used to mask or obscure such political responses.

We know that human beings are social animals. We live together in various types of social groupings and gain our sense of identity and self-esteem within social contexts. The social arrangements are numerous, but it is only the rare individual who genuinely prefers no social interaction at all, and even hermits are products of a particular previous social environment. If true hermits do exist, they only prove the rule that all human actions and decisions are made in particular social contexts.

Human individuals are nurtured, for better or worse, in particular social environments and tend to internalize the values of that social grouping. These values, in turn, emerge out of the history of the particular group. Values are products of communal existence and demonstrate the human need for community maintenance. Human values are one aspect of species survival strategy. They are encapsulations of the survival techniques of particular social groups.

If no values can claim a transcendent source, are all values relative and of equal worth? Does this not lead directly to nihilism and underscore the poverty of the type of historical-critical analysis in which we are engaged? Is it not impossible to commit ourselves to anything once we have agreed that all values are human creations, one no less so than another?

There is certainly a sense in which this is true. Values, morals, restrictions and taboos, by the very fact that they have emerged out of communal existence, have represented at one point or another in the history of that community a successful survival strategy. If this were not the case, either the values would not have been adopted or the community would have perished. Therefore, while we must reject the notion that any particular value or set of values has come to human communities from a transcendent source, it is equally clear that in particular social situations some values are useful and positive and other values have become stagnantly dysfunctional. The advocacy of particular values reflects the desire to elicit certain moral and political responses within particular social situations. Therefore, in the discussion of such values we must be willing to define and defend the moral and political responses wanted, and not use values language to mask or obscure such responses.

As historical situations change, values may become stagnant and counterproductive. Successful survival strategies from one period of a group's history, embodied in a particular set of values, morals, restrictions and taboos, may bring disaster when applied to new historical circumstances. If that group cannot adopt new values, the people may perish.[4]

Because we live as a species in radically new circumstances, circumstances in which our survival as a species is at stake if we continue to hold fast to the values of our culture that have

brought us to this precipice, we must be willing to critically examine even our most cherished assumptions. This includes especially assumptions expressed in sacrosanct terms, such as human
nature and God. This is the context out of which all serious religious probing must be pursued. The task of religious reflection
is, therefore, one in which questioning and testing is essential.[5]
Particular models of God elicit identifiable moral and political
responses within particular social situations. We must be willing
to define and defend those moral and political responses and not
allow traditional ideas of God to mask or obscure them.

* * *

Human existence is grounded in the physical world. Survival
in the physical world is the bottom line of our being. But we are
much more than physical beings. Humans have powers of mind,
of reasoning and ability to learn, which extend far beyond what
is necessary for mere physical survival. This mental overload is
the source of our creativity and is expressed in our intuition that
human beings have a soul and spirit as well as a physical body.

The *human soul* and *human spirit* are not exact terms—even
less concrete than the related word, *mind*. For mind connotes
mental activity and that can be located in a specific organ of the
body, the brain.[6] To speak of the human soul and human spirit,
on the other hand, is to speak of aspects of the human being
thought of in ordinary terms as in distinction to the physical body.
It is to speak of that aspect of human thought and experience that
seems to transcend and fly far above the physical world.

We speak of the soul and spirit, working together through
the mind, as the seat of human creativity and aesthetic sensitiv-
ity. Working within the physical world, we seek to arrange what
is found there so that it bears the mark of our personality. We
arrange words into poems. We arrange sounds into music. We
shape wood and stone into works of art and fine craftsmanship.
We arrange the natural order into gardens and parks. Recognition of the creative ability of human beings to shape the natural
order into expressions of the human personality is surely why, in
every age, the work of the artist and craftsperson has been held
in high esteem. One can find no instrumental reason why a particular painting, for example, should be valued higher than a
house. The representation itself becomes the artist's or craftsperson's real act of transcendent (from *beyond*) religious conviction.

It is through the soul and spirit that we come to appreciate the works of creativity we see in others. A purely intellectual analysis of, for example, a piece of music, is possible. It may be profound in its depths, including the physics of vibration and the correspondence of harmony patterns to aspects of the human nervous system. But for most of us, this will never quite express what we hear in that music—the communication of joy, emotion, the sense of release. While our attempts to speak of such things are necessarily fluid and imprecise, I do think we can say that this *something more* we recognize and appreciate when we encounter works of human creativity points toward what we mean by the human soul and the human spirit. This is perhaps also why, when we look at a beautiful sunset, the power of a gleaming waterfall, or examine the intricate structure of a living thing, it is most easy for us to encounter that beauty in terms of appreciation for a creative world spirit.

Closely related to the work of the soul and spirit in creating and appreciating beauty, that which bears the mark of our personality, is our ability to love. Giving and receiving love is the highest expression of human creativity, of that toward which we point when we speak of the human soul and the human spirit. Love breaks through the protective barriers we erect around ourselves in fear and mistrust. It is through love that we most clearly know ourselves as a unity of body, soul, and spirit. It is through love that we are able to direct most positively our creative energies. It is through love that our creative works are lifted up and invested with meaning and significance far beyond that which an intellectual analysis of those works could convey.

This is strikingly expressed in one of the most beautiful biblical passages, chapter 13 of the apostle Paul's letter to the Corinthian community. Speaking of our creative and spiritual gifts, the passage insists that without love, they come to nothing. Here love is described as always patient and kind. Love is never jealous, boastful, or conceited. Love is always ready to trust and hope. Our greatest gifts as human beings, that toward which we ultimately point when we speak of the human soul and human spirit, are faith, hope, and love. And of these, love is the greatest, the best, the most perfect.

Those aspects of the human experience that cannot be reduced simply to the physical, although of course they are rooted in the physical,[7] are what we point to when we speak of the human soul and the human spirit. Creativity, transcendence, and love best summarize the works of the soul and spirit. These are what we cherish most about being human. These are what give us the sense of being *special* in the order of nature. Our animal siblings do not appear to possess aptitudes of creativity, transcendence, and love in any degree approaching that of human beings. For this reason we rightly distinguish and set ourselves, our species, apart from other species.

* * *

But we also know that there is something terribly wrong with us as human beings. The very aspect of our being that sets us apart from our animal siblings, which sets us *above* the natural order, is also a source of our shame and disgrace as a species. Many of our animal siblings kill out of instinct and for food. But we humans kill for the purely sadistic joy of killing. Our animal siblings may stand by while a fellow suffers out of helplessness and lack of understanding. But humans purposely inflict suffering on other humans and other species, understanding full well what is happening, and watch that suffering with Mephistophelian fascination.

The real possibility of our extinction as a species, and many other species with us, comes neither from our mother the earth nor from our animal siblings, no matter how savage and wild. It comes from us, ourselves, the crown of the natural order. That which sets us apart from the rest of the natural order, the human soul and spirit, the very source of our ability to create, transcend, and love, also sets a raging whirlwind in our breasts which leads us, daemonically enchanted, toward species extinction. That by which we may reach so high has also cursed us to sink so low. That which can and should be our source of creativity, transcendence and love too often becomes our source of shame and debasement in the visage of the natural order.

For the human being is a self-contradictory animal. In our minds we are truly divine beings, transcendent and ethereal. In our minds we can create new worlds or sit on the far side of the moon. Yet this divine, transcendent, ethereal human soul and spirit is entirely dependent on a weak and mortal physical body. After we, in our creative imaginations, have created new worlds and sat on the far side of the moon, we must inevitably return and attend to a physical body, a body that hungers and thirsts, defecates, becomes ill, and finally dies, taking our soul and spirit with it. A divine being who is that vulnerable! No wonder there is a raging whirlwind in our breasts.

We are indeed a curious race. Tied to a weak and mortal physical body, we spend most of our psychic energy in the creation of symbols of immortality, which allows us, through vicarious identification, at least momentarily to suppress from consciousness the fact of who we really are. Our revered symbols, both sacred and secular, all point toward higher allegiances, toward that which is solid, eternal, and whole, toward that which is, unlike ourselves, heroic and immortal. Our strivings are toward, as Ernest Becker saw so clearly, a denial of death.[8]

This contradiction in our very being is what the great religious traditions point to in the metaphor of the *fallen* state of the human condition. A pervasive and intuitive awareness extends through time and across cultures that there is something desperately wrong with us as people. We die, and in our fallen state the sting of death is painful indeed.

As far as we know, we are the only species that knows and understands the fact of death years before it actually happens. Some of our animal siblings never seem to understand death, even as the predator pounces or the butcher's blade is poised for the kill. Other of our animal siblings do seem to experience a kind of terror in the moments just before the mortal blow. We have all been haunted by that look of terror on an animal face. But we human beings must live with that furious terror within us, now simmering, now boiling, from relatively early childhood until the day the death angel calls.

* * *

Taming this terror is, quite literally, *the* most important human task. If the terror could not be tamed, forward movement would simply be impossible. The person would be psychotically stunned and unable to act. Fortunately, in all but the most tragic cases, a more or less successful process of taming does occur. This taming takes one of two paths: the path of acceptance or the path of denial.

Along both paths, the mechanism for taming the terror of death awareness is to create symbols of immortality, of solidity and strength, with which the person can identify and thus through which the person vicariously participates in immortality. There, however, the similarity ends. For the one taking the path of acceptance, the symbols chosen as aids in the taming process are exactly those which help with internalizing and incorporating awareness of the self as being-toward-death. It may often be a goal for those who have chosen this path to arrive at the point where substitutionary symbols of immortality might be abandoned altogether.

The path of acceptance, of incorporation of death-consciousness into the soul and spirit, is paradoxically the path leading to life, to a natural flowing of creativity, transcendent awareness, and love. This path allows human beings to maximize their potential on the earth. As will be seen, this is the path toward which Jesus of Nazareth and other great religious figures pointed, and is the only way to make sense of the recurring paradox appearing in one form or another in all of the world's religions and great literature—that to have life, one must first lose it.

The path of denial leads in a fundamentally opposite direction. Along this path, acceptance of death awareness is rejected and displaced by identification with symbols of power. Because death is encountered as an ultimate limitation, those choosing the path of denial opt for an *ersatz* reality, channeling their denial into systems and schemes of domination over nature and other human beings.

Nietzsche, a philosopher who understood the terror of the human situation as did few others, extolled this as the will to power and domination.[9] By dominating others, one denies mortality by creating the illusion of *being more* (i.e., more being!) than those others whom one dominates. From childish one-upmanship games to the full-blown hierarchical structure of a tyrannical empire, the path of denial perverts the work of the human soul and spirit. Creativity becomes destructive, while love is replaced by defensiveness, fear and suspicion. It is a zero-sum game in which gains in self-respect and life-enhancement for some must necessarily be bought by oppression and deprecation of others. "Eat or be eaten" is the underlying ethic of this path.

Far from holding its symbols of immortality as tentative, as aids for spiritual growth that may finally be abandoned, those taking the path of denial are forced to hold ever more tightly to their symbols, insisting on their objective and universal nature. To let go would quite literally mean death for them. Their immortality symbols become idols in the most definite sense. They are a human creation to which their creators then willingly sacrifice themselves and others.[10] In fact, the more sacrifices demanded to maintain the effectiveness of such symbols, the more sacred they become.

The path of denial is ultimately the path of death. It creates illusions of super humanness that are no more real than the power of idols. Yet those taking this path must quite literally invest their entire being in maintaining these illusions. They can only be maintained on the backs of others, thus destroying true freedom and community even while maintaining order, and ultimately consume their own creators.

Those choosing the path of denial are often bound to what might be characterized as a social sadomasochistic ritual, dominating in one sphere and being dominated in another: toadying up to the boss at work and then lording over weaker family members at home. Along the path of denial, this constitutes the everyday world for most people.[11]

Along this path, the more encompassing the symbol of immortality, the more dangerous and daemonic it becomes. For competing symbols of immortality must inevitably clash, with each other and with reality. People participating in an immortality symbol must finally abandon it or sacrifice themselves. The more encompassing the immortality symbol, the grander will be the sacrificial resources gathered to maintain it.

During the Cold War, the clash of great symbols of immortality, symbols we labeled without any sense of irony as superpowers, threatened us and many other species with extinction.[12] Although it appears one side finally "won" this conflict, the winners find now that they are so psychologically addicted to weapons of mass destruction for their very self-image they are unable to disarm or even significantly cut their overwhelming spending on even more weapons of war, even in face of the obvious historical experience that the holding of weapons such as these by one nation will only stimulate the desire of other nations also to maintain such arsenals. Many of their leading politicians now clamor for a renewed space-based defense initiative, at costs that cannot even be credibly estimated (including unilateral scrapping of the meager international weapons treaties that do exist) to fight against foes and enemies they cannot even name.

The path of denial is the easier one. It is the path that becomes normal during our society's socialization process. As we learn to be good citizens, we accept and with religious devotion internalize, as our own immortality symbols, those symbols our society offers to us: the nation, the party, success, material acquisition. We accept the structural hierarchy, exploitation, and oppression of others, of our environment, and of ourselves. Such acceptance is necessary to maintain the convincing authority of these structures. In the everyday world, this subservience and the sacrifices it demands is not even noticed, much less seriously questioned.

But a few have been inadequately socialized or because of some other stimulus have questioned social fictions by which society imparts the momentary security of the path of denial to its members. Many of these people have been judged insane or worse. But they have had an insight that the rest of us, at this juncture in our evolutionary development, must take seriously. Those who have stood against the hierarchy, exploitation, and oppression of particular social constructions must become our teachers. Those who have taken the path of acceptance rather than denial must become our guides. Those who have found socially independent resources for meaning that have allowed them to move forward in life without reliance on destructive immortality symbols must become our tutors. [13]

Are there socially independent resources of meaning, sources of spiritual strength, for taming the terror of the human condition in a constructive and loving manner? These are questions that focus religious reflection on the nature and reality of God.

Excursive Update—I have been struggling to find a meaningful way to communicate what for the past twenty years or so has been a deep intuition that the human soul and spirit must be conceived as fully embodied and that, while conceptually distinct from material body, the soul and spirit cannot be separated in any meaningful way from the body. The intuitive image I hold in my mind's eye is that of campfire, in which the fire is conceptually distinct from the wood, yet any attempt to separate the fire from the wood results in nothing but dead wood. I am not at all satisfied with materialistic reductionism, which suggests in effect that the fire of the soul and spirit are merely ephemeral and that hardcore reality is the dead wood. At the same time, I am thoroughly convinced that the concept of fire apart from the wood is a major category error.

Recently I became aware of two streams of interpretation that give a very firm grounding to these intuitions. The first of these is the work of George Lakoff and Mark Johnson.[14] The basic intent of their project is to think philosophically within a context of fully digesting the last twenty-some years of cognitive science and linguistics research. They demonstrate convincingly that human reasoning and abstract thinking (i.e., the higher functioning associated with the human spiritual nature) is built up through linguistic metaphor, from very basic body-based experiences. Research in cognitive development suggests that our most basic physical experiences are registered in a set of neural pathways, which then connect up with myriad other neural-linguistic pathways in the formation of abstract thought. Human reasoning is built up from the same types of thought processes that other animal species experience.

However, human mental processes are able to reflect upon these experiences at a much more complex level and become shaped by specific cultural-linguistic patterns. Reasoning and emotions are not separate mental faculties, but are mutually interactive and interdependent activities of the brain. The most basic categories of metaphor and oppositions,[15] on which all higher reasoning and communication are based, are fundamentally rooted in physical, bodily experience generated over time and contouring the entire process of mental development. An intelligence formed in some other way (e.g., an artificially programmed intelligence) simply will not have the same kind of reasoning patterns as human body-based intelligence.

The second stream of interpretation is the "nonreductive physicalism" being explored and developed especially by Nancey Murphy and her colleagues at Fuller Theological Seminary.[16] In this view, it is granted that the higher human mental capacities (including spiritual aptitude) are "emergent properties" built up from processes fully contained within the physical field of functioning. However, this view insists that once such properties emerge, they can no longer legitimately be reduced to the physical functioning from which they emerged nor be described exhaustively by describing those physical processes.

Such emergent properties introduce a fresh element into the picture. To return to my intuitive image of the campfire, once the logs are ignited, there is a genuinely new element in the picture that was not there the split second before combustion occurred, though combustion could not have taken place in any meaningful sense apart from the conditions present just before combustion, and the new element in the picture (fire) cannot be understood or investigated in any meaningful sense apart from the continuing fuel that feeds it.

In both of these streams of interpretation, there is a yet-to-be solved problem of when, in the developmental histories of individuals and of the species, this new element of recognizably human higher functioning appears and what might be the catalyst for its appearance. This is the point at which these streams of interpretation, in my view, potentially connect with and could be extended by the theoretical work of Ernest Becker, which I have called the *theory of generative mortality anxiety*. There is a point at which the human brain appears to begin a nascent reflection on its own processes—that is, becomes aware of itself as an entity existing in the world. It is at this point that a catalyst becomes operative and further mental development begins to move at an exponential pace, after which we clearly are dealing with a recognizably human, higher functioning element.

It appears logical here to suggest that death awareness and the ensuing development of a dynamic unconscious containing powerfully repressed material is a strong candidate for what this catalyst might be. Or if the catalyst is something else, generative mortality anxiety must be, at the very least, one of the most elemental psychological compounds formed by that catalyst.

2

THE AMBIGUITY OF EVIL

*I*f the recent century taught us anything, it was that the reality of human evil, the depths of the human capacity for sin and destructiveness, cannot be minimized. Notions once current in the Western world, assuming the inevitability of human moral progress, are now destroyed beyond repair. Faith in progress dies hard for Americans, for whom it is all but inseparable from national character. America was founded on the faith of the Enlightenment. Optimism about human possibilities has been an integral part of that faith. If Augustinian or Calvinistic concepts of original sin sobered the Founding Fathers enough to prevent the rise of an American version of the Jacobins, the combination of deistic free thinkers and religious auto-inspirationists put the Tories in a small minority. Among those attending the First Continental Congress, even the conservatives were radical by any standard of that time.

To speak of doubt about innate human goodness and human progress is to speak of doubt about America's mission in the world and in human history. It is almost enough to raise questions about one's national patriotism! Indeed, even today, on this side of two world wars, and amid the resurgent patriotism after September 11, 2001, an essay like Denis de Rougemont's *On the Devil and Politics* rings strange to American ears.[1]

The progressive perfecting of the human race through enlightened reason was an integral tenet of the religious and humanistic liberalism of the nineteenth and early twentieth centuries. Human evil was characterized as intolerance, disease,

41

tyranny and inequality, the root cause of which was ignorance. Such evil would be overcome by reason through education. In that view, humanity could face the future with confident optimism. The old Calvinistic doctrine of human depravity was not so much refuted as simply ignored, even among Calvinists.

This kind of optimism, in both its religious and secular forms, has been very attractive to Americans. It embodies democracy and good old Yankee know-how. Even those who continued to preach sin and depravity narrowed their focus of human evil to the level of personal transgressions, such as drink, gambling, dancing, and adultery. On a social level, it made no sense to insist on pessimism and at the same time participate enthusiastically in the spread of American democracy and capitalism.

The subsequent years of the twentieth century and into the twenty-first brought two world wars, the rise of Nazism and Fascism, the murders of Stalin and Pol Pot, the attempted genocide against the Jewish people, Hiroshima and Nagasaki, the Cold War and the arms race, the Vietnam War, the atrocities in Serbia and Bosnia, Ethiopia and Rwanda, the still-unfolding consequences of September 11, not to mention global warming and other harbingers of ecological disaster. The undeniable reality of human depravity and evil has returned to us with a vengeance. Any religious reflection adequate to our time cannot minimize this evil or simply ignore it and continue to applaud the divine goodness of human nature.

* * *

Sigmund Freud was among the first of those thinkers who were originally committed to the Enlightenment worldview who slowly began to see how deeply rooted destructiveness and evil really are in the human heart. Freud claimed that the goal of his science of psychoanalysis was to replace Id with Ego, to replace unconsciously motivated drives and actions with actions more under the guidance of conscious reasoning. But the longer Freud delved into the human soul, the more pessimistic he became about human prospects. Building on Freud, but also moving considerably beyond Freud in incorporating sociological and social-theoretical sources, various thinkers have produced a sophisticated phenomenology of human evil which now must be taken seriously in any useful religious reflection on the human situation.[2]

As was seen in the previous chapter, this phenomenological approach very soon leads us to see that *human nature is split*. We are godlike in our mental world, yet tied to death and decay in the physical world. Consciousness of death makes us extremely anxious beings. We calm that fear by bonding to that which gives a sense of permanence and eternality.

According to this basic insight concerning the nature of being human, we all want to endure and prosper and in some sense gain immortality. Knowing that we are mortal, but needing to repress that knowledge from immediate consciousness, we mask the recognition of mortality. We suppress awareness of it through the creation of an emotional, psychological, and spiritual investment in complex symbols of immortality. In turn, our symbols give us what we seek, which is immunity from mortality (or at least a functioning illusion of it.) According to Ernest Becker, in my view the best representative of the post-Freudian, phenomenological tradition, this flight from mortality is perhaps the most important driving force behind human evil.

> The thing that makes [humankind] the most devastating animal that ever stuck his neck up into the sky is that he wants a stature and a destiny that is impossible for an animal; he wants an earth that is not an earth but a heaven, and the price for this kind of fantastic ambition is to make the earth an even more eager graveyard than it naturally is.[3]

Becker employed a central concept, borrowed from the literature of anthropology, which helps us understand the dynamic behind human evil—the concept of fetishism. Fetishism has various meanings, but in this context it designates a process by which one thing is initially used to symbolize another, then is eventually treated as the thing itself.

For example, wealth can objectively be described as a relatively abundant command of goods and services. The pursuit of wealth would then mean the pursuit and accumulation of goods and services. Money is a symbol for goods and services or for the power to command goods and services. The pursuit of wealth therefore might logically take the course of the pursuit of money. However, the pursuit of money (thousands, millions, and now billions!) very easily becomes an end in itself, something invested with psychological power only secondarily having to do with goods and services. It becomes something pursued for itself. It becomes a fetish.

Fetishism connotes a *narrowing down* that has become irrational. The pursuit of wealth in the form of goods and services can be seen as rational, as a part of survival, although it would surely also then have a rational satiation point. But the pursuit of money for its own sake, as a fetishistic symbol of wealth, has no satiation point. You can always add more zeros to the ledger. Who can say they really have enough? There is a self-sacrificial element inherent in fetishism as well, and as any family counselor will readily attest, the first thing sacrificed in the pursuit of money is our family lives and our marriages. For as with idolatry, that which we ourselves construct becomes the consuming focus of our life energies and we therefore miss the truly available richness of life's experience. Life becomes too narrow and constricted.

Some degree of narrowing down is necessary to human life. There is too much possible experience in any given moment not to narrow down. Even alone in one room, it would be impossible to describe fully all that it is possible to experience in that room. We inevitably must narrow down our awareness, and for the most part only those things that are pragmatically useful come to our attention. Most of what is actually going on passes us by without conscious notice. Our conscious minds are simply not capable of taking in all that reality has to offer. A mind unable to narrow down at all would be stunned by the multiplicity of everyday life.

This is even more obviously the case when we bring into view other human beings. It becomes impossible to take in all that is there to experience in the personality, the character, the individuality of each person. Just to look closely into the eyes of one other person can be momentarily immobilizing. Our minds are not capable of taking in all that other people have to offer. A mind unable to narrow down at all, to notice some things and exclude other things from notice, would be stunned by the multiplicity of experience of other people.

But how narrowly must we narrow down? To experience life too narrowly is crippling. To experience a landscape only in terms of a prospective development site is crippling. To experience another human being only in terms of being a prospective client, or customer, or consumer, or in terms of his or her sexual organs, is crippling. It is to miss even the available fullness of life that we, with our limited capacity, are able to experience.

* * *

It is difficult to arrive at an agreed-upon definition of evil. But from the ways evil has been symbolized in human history, it is very easy to see that it is always closely associated with death and decay, or, in a word, mortality. Across time and cultures, in its many forms and by its many names, evil personified is represented by symbols of animality, death, and decay.[4] Typically, the Christian Satan (though as Lucifer, once considered an angel of light) is pictured with animal characteristics, such as horns, hoofs, and tail. Satan's abode is Gehenna, the place of the dead. The smell is of putrification and feces. Satan's surroundings are filled with skulls and bones, vipers, dirt, and filth. Satan is totally immersed in the physical world of sexual lust.

Evil comes to contain a very clear moral sense as well. Satan is above all wicked, the arch-enemy and opponent of good, of God. But this has not always been the case, for God also has not always had such a clearly defined moral character. Even in the most ancient of the biblical literature, hints and echoes remain of a time when Satan was seen as Azazel, the god of the wilderness, a different god from Israel's God, but not necessarily evil (cf. Lev. 16). God and Satan, good and evil, were seen as opposing but complementary aspects of reality, perhaps something like the concept of *yin/yang* in Oriental philosophy.

With the development of settled civilization, God, the good, began to have a more clearly defined moral character. Likewise evil, that which was contrary to the good, to civilization, also began to have a very defined moral character. Evil was seen as opposition to the will of God, as acting contrary to the law of God, as contrary to the good of society. Evil was seen as wickedness, as disorder and chaos. The symbols used to describe incarnated evil, Satan or the Devil, confirm the meaning of evil as death and decay, as mortality itself.

Our aversion to evil is rooted in the attempt to escape mortality. But at the same time, as Ernest Becker noted, the flight from mortality is the root of human evil. In reflecting on this paradox, that both good and evil are rooted in the selfsame desire to escape mortality/evil, we are on to something crucial.

We oppose evil, and rightly so. There are very few among us who consciously embrace evil. Those who do are rightly considered to be clinically pathological. The tradition of liberal human-

ism was to that extent correct when it assumed the natural goodness of human beings—that under normal circumstances people
would choose the good and oppose evil.

Reality, however, is too much for us to take in. We must narrow it down. Likewise, mortality is too much for us to oppose.
And so also we unconsciously narrow evil down. Mortality cannot be opposed. *But lawbreakers can!* There is nothing we can do
to halt death. But *this* enemy (pick a random enemy from the
pages of the history books to fill in the blank . . .) we can defeat!

The basic theory here is not obscure or difficult to understand. In our opposition to evil, we must of necessity narrow and
focus on specific evils. Specific evils we can do something about.
Our motives are good, and it is certainly better that specific evils
be opposed than that no evils be opposed. However, our tendency is to fetishize specific evils, to become too narrow in our
focus, as if all will be well if we can just conquer this specific evil
before us. Every war soon (even, perhaps especially, a war on terrorism) becomes a war to end all wars.

This is especially dangerous when we consider another
fetishist urge, that of scapegoating, of identifying our narrowly
focused evil of evils with particular persons, groups, races, and
ideologies.[5] Once that happens, we quickly loose any ability to
place limits on our violence in eradicating evil. Who can place
limits on what we must be willing to do in fighting against *Evil
Itself*? From there it is a very short step to identifying the eradica-
tion of this evil with *God's cause*, at which point massacre becomes
a sacramental act![6] Once this dynamic is combined with the tech-
nical ability to execute mass destruction and the stage is thus set
for the treacheries and demonic acts of the twentieth and twenty-
first centuries.

Because this is so integral to the overall religious perspective
I want to present here, let me emphasize concisely once again
what this theory of human evil contends. In seeking to fight
against evil, humans bring ever more evil into the world, because
all but inevitably the evil we fight against has been too narrowly
defined and too narrowly focused on other human beings and
other human ideologies. As Ernest Becker put it,

> But if we add together the logic of the heroic [struggle
> against evil] with the necessary fetishization of evil, we get
> a formula that is no longer pathetic but terrifying. It ex-
> plains almost by itself why [the human being], of all ani-

mals, has caused the most devastation on earth—the most real evil. [The human being] alone struggles extra hard to be immune to death because he alone is conscious of it; but by being able to identify and isolate evil arbitrarily, he is capable of lashing out in all directions against imagined dangers of this world. . . . [The human being] is an animal who must fetishize to survive and to have 'normal mental health.' But this shrinkage of vision that permits him to survive also at the same time prevents him from having the overall understanding he needs to plan for and control the effects of his shrinkage of experience.[7]

This is the most frightening thing about the ambiguity of human evil. We commit our most evil acts out of heroic intentions, the very desire to eradicate evil. Military generals and public executioners always see themselves as working toward the good on both sides of any conflict. People from Germany confidently repeated *"Gott Mit Uns"* while the Allies were just as sure that God was on their side. In the Middle East warring parties perennially invoke God and the rightness of their cause while charging the other with terrorism.

It is no wonder that we have had trouble accepting the doctrine of human depravity and have only had its undeniable truth more or less forced upon us by the accumulation of recent human atrocities. For when we examine ourselves, what we find is not at all a desire to hurt, maim, and slay, except for those few poor souls who are truly clinically pathological. What we find is the intention to struggle heroically against evil and for the good.

Human beings will identify as an *enemy* that which potentially threatens personal expansion or that of the group. A fascinating book illustrating this dynamic is Sam Keen's *Faces of the Enemy*.[8] In this book, a study of wartime propaganda, including many pages of wartime and revolutionary propaganda posters, Keen outlines a number of ways in which the enemy is fetishized and characterized as that which is fearful, threatening, and in need of extermination.

In what Keen calls the archetypes of the enemy, we find an impressive array of images. We find the enemy characterized as the *stranger*, the outsider to our group, THEM versus US. The enemy becomes the *aggressor*, the guilty one in the conflict. The enemy is the *faceless one*, who is therefore not human. The enemy is characterized as the *enemy of God*, by which he is made to seem demonic. There is the enemy as *barbarian*, the threat to order and culture. The enemy is *greedy*, lusting after more territory and conquest. The enemy is likened to a *criminal*, the perpetrator of terrorism and lawbreaking. As *torturer and rapist*, the enemy is sadistic violator. Pictured as *beast, reptile, insect, or germ*, the enemy is seen as fit only for extermination. Finally, and most significantly, in pictures of skulls, bones, and gravekeepers, the enemy is likened eventually to *death itself*. Although Keen focuses mainly on overt propaganda posters, one unfortunately need go no farther than the political cartoons of most any daily newspaper to find exactly parallel examples of these faces of the enemy.

* * *

In light of this modern phenomenology of human evil, the apostle Paul's words take on new significance. "For it is not against flesh and blood that we wrestle, but against principalities and powers. . . " (Eph. 6). We wrestle against the power of culture to define our enemies for us, against the monopoly of society to transmit to us for our consumption fetishized images of evil that are too narrowly construed—and therefore lead us into becoming unwitting perpetrators of ever more human evil. In light of this modern phenomenology of human evil, *wrestling with principalities and powers* must mean the process of rigorous self-criticism whereby we come to see the definitions of our culture as relative, or even as downright lies, and strive to flush these prejudices from our attitudes and actions.

We must be bold in naming these powers and struggling against them. Certainly *unjust economic systems* are one of these structures which would have us believe we have a *right* to the resources and wealth of others because we pay for them, and that the economic hopes and ambitions of others are a threat to these rights. *Militarism* is one of the strongest of the powers. Militarism, which begins in a legitimate urge for protection, forces on us constructions of reality that lead to dividing the world into armed camps.

Racism, sexism, and (as we are seeing of late in church bodies across the nation) *homophobia* also carry the power to have us falsely define evil in our world and therefore falsely divide ourselves against each other.

The *media* in American culture are clearly a power equal to militarism in potentially demonic force. The media more than anything else transmit to us those cultural images of what is good and evil. In the grips of the system of *profit-maximization* (which itself fetishizes reality irrationally in obvious ways) the media decide what we will see and how we will see it on a scale more massive than at any time in human history. Hiding behind the chimera of objectivity, and the excuse that "We only give people what they want," our televisions pipe in a constant and daily dose of glamorized violence and killing aimed not only at adults but, what is surely criminal, at our teenagers and children.[9] Stories and facts contradicting the official line on world events are systematically ignored as unworthy of the news.

Especially in America, *consumerism*, the urge for *always bigger and better*, is another definite power. Spurred by advertising, the life-blood of the mass media, people are made to feel restless and dissatisfied with what they have and to want ever more, even in a country that by any stretch of measurement is the most materially prosperous in history. As with the alcoholic drinking himself to death, this urge for more must be satiated even as the resulting destruction of the environment, which is a direct result, threatens to make large areas of our land uninhabitable. The happiness consumerism offers turns out not to be fulfillment at all—but a treadmill pursuit of an ever receding aspiration point. Greed, once considered one of the deadly vices, is now openly extolled as a virtue in our culture. Children are taught to admire and seek to imitate heroes not for the content of their character but for the color of their green.

What effect does this have for serious religious reflection? At the close of the last chapter we stood seeking personal sources of meaning and spiritual strength; that is, we stood before the problem of God. Has this detour, in which we have attempted to confront the reality of human evil, derailed our venture? I think not, but it should certainly sober us to the arduousness of our task. Those gods most easily invoked are projections of mainstream cultural values who preside over our heroic but evil deeds. Therefore, before we are ready to speak of God, we need yet to make explicit the parameters our confrontation with human evil sets for our discussion.

We know we have the tendency to define too narrowly the focus of evil. Among other things, this leads us to see the *demonic* in the face of the enemy. We know that a narrowing down of the multiplicity of experience is necessary for forward movement.

But it is a necessary tendency we must necessarily resist whenever we become aware of it. *Any invocation of God that appears to justify our demonization of other human beings must be treated with absolute suspicion. Those gods that aid us in expanding our vision of reality, which lead us to reconcile ourselves to those from whom we have been alienated, those whom we have seen as Other, must be given privileged consideration.* A true God leads one to self-criticism, a wrestling with principalities and powers, and not to simple affirmation of oneself in one's prejudices and confirmation of one's myopia.[10]

* * *

I stated in the introduction that the most obvious moral influence I retain from my Mennonite background is a strong commitment to pacifism. As a thinking adult, I now commit to that stand on grounds much more complex than those I was taught during my upbringing. In the context of the present analysis, we are now able to make sense of at least part of that adult commitment.

We know that we have an heroic urge to move against evil. But we also know that we have a necessary drive to define evil in narrow and manageable channels. This leads us to identify evil with the ideologies, actions and being of other concrete human beings. In this we are greatly influenced by the Pauline principalities and powers of cultural transmission. In short, we can never be sure in any absolute sense that what we have identified as evil and those whom we have identified as evil are in fact evil, and not simply our fetishistic illusion of evil. In fact, all of history points us toward the conclusion that we are probably wrong, and that our move against the evil we see will simply lead to further evil.

Yet it would be wrong simply to throw up our hands and give the sanction of silence to the evil we see. We need to move against evil, but must struggle to do so in ways that make it least likely that we will thereby add to the evil that already exists. Much work has been done on nonviolence as a philosophically committed political tactic, and much more yet needs to be done to elucidate clearly before a skeptical world how this approach could work in resisting evil in the politic realm.[11] In the meantime I want to say that for me, pacifism means, above all else, a sort of political application of the Hippocratic maxim, "Above all, do no harm." In other words, at that point in our struggle against evil when we would feel justified to kill, maim or slay another human being, signal flags should stand out on our mental horizon, warning us that we have constricted our view of evil too narrowly and have scapegoated the cause of evil too myopically.

It is at this point that self-criticism is needed, that we must further wrestle with principalities and powers, before we are ready to resume the struggle against evil. Failure to do so at this point will inevitably lead us into becoming perpetrators of yet another of the atrocities of human history. To act as a pacifist in the move against evil, to commit categorically to nonviolent means in the struggle against evil, does not in itself guarantee that we will always see evil clearly and without self-righteous distortion, but at least this makes it much less likely that we will commit irreparable atrocities in our struggle against evil.[12]

Only a God who helps us to expand our vision, who leads us toward reconciliation with the enemy, who assists us in the task of self-criticism, in wrestling with the principalities and powers of our world, is worthy of committed attention in our contemporary world.

Excursive Update—I want to connect my reflections in this chapter directly to the important work on *The Powers* done by theologian and biblical scholar Walter Wink.[12] I had opportunity to present in seminar form most of the material contained in this chapter at a conference in March 2000, sponsored by Eastern Mennonite University and focused on Wink's work. Based on the interaction I had with Wink and others following this seminar, I am quite comfortable with the suggestion that I am describing in language informed primarily by social science and social theory the same phenomena that in Wink's work is delineated primarily in biblical and theological categories. It is significant that the common ground for action in the world between these two approaches turns out to be an *a priori* commitment to nonviolence.[14]

3

GOD IN THE
NEXUS OF HUMAN HISTORY

*P*robing questions of ultimate concern, of meaning, of human spirituality, are always intricately connected to religion and the concept of God. The human condition places a heavy burden on us of fashioning meaning for our lives out of the raw data of personal and collective experience.

In light of this reality, we see why exploration of the concept of God is a universal urge for human beings. For in whatever simple or complex notions God is conceived, God represents, at a minimum, a vision of a perfect being. God is a concept expressing what it would be like to have creative and transcending mental and spiritual characteristics, rather than being simultaneously limited by the human characteristic of physical mortality and frailty. Whatever else God might be, God is our highest immortality symbol.[1]

God resolves the contradiction we human beings feel within us. We are split beings, feeling our fallen imperfection. God is whole, perfect. Whatever else God might be, the concept of God springs from the transcending human mind, a creative expression of the solution to the human dilemma. God is conceived as the human spirit's ultimate goal in the quest for creating meaning in the human situation. We come closest to picturing a person's deepest emotional, spiritual and psychological yearning when we encounter that person's image of God.

* * *

Because the concept of God emerges from our quest for meaning and wholeness, it follows most naturally that one of the ways in which we picture God is as *Creator*. Integral to the quest for meaning and wholeness is a satisfying answer to the question, "From where do we come?" We are historical beings. The meaning we find in human community cannot be separated from knowledge that our present is grounded in a significant past.

On the personal level, we see this spiritual quest in the search for family roots, the current interest in genealogical research. Traditional communities have their storytellers and keepers of the communal legends and ancestral chronicles. In traditional societies, there is not much need for personal histories, since each individual member of society in immerged in the collective narrative of the group. It is not surprising that in modern, atomized societies, in which traditional human connections are strained and broken by the pace of modern living, the genealogist is kept most busy. When participation in the social community itself is no longer able to inspire a deep sense of purpose, many people seek to find that sense of being grounded in personal family history.

On the collective level, the historians of modern societies work to create national or cultural narratives that enhance the sense of historical mission in a particular community or nation, its sense of a purposeful past. Our best historians are those who are able to weave an inclusive pattern of coherent narrative meaning from the factoids of the past without simply producing uncritical hagiography.

At an even more abstract level, the evolutionary scientist seeks to unlock the mystery of the origins of species, of the earth and the universe itself. Difficult as it may be at times to follow the intricate reasoning of these scholars and scientists, there are very few among us who have no interest in the museum exhibits and media programs that follow from this type of research. That so many of our most gifted people, consistently in generation after generation, devote their lives to this research is clear evidence of the vital importance we place on the question "From where?" for our construction of a sense of meaning, wholeness and purpose.

But we want more than this. Understanding the mechanism of evolution can only go so far in satisfying the quest of the soul and spirit for meaning, wholeness and a sense of purpose. We seek an answer qualitatively different from that which the magnificent theories of science can provide. It is in answer to this qualitatively different question that the meaning of the attribute of God as Creator is found. It is not simply as answer to yet another round of the child's question, "Then where did that come from?" that human beings are led to ponder the concept of God as Creator. Ascribing the attribute of Creator to our concept of God is, rather, the exclamation of the human soul and spirit that we do find partial and fleeting but nonetheless significant intimations of meaning, wholeness and purpose in this universe, in our mother the earth, in human community and in our individual lives. In these fleeting, partial, but nonetheless significant intimations of meaning, wholeness and purpose, there is an unmistakable feeling of gratitude, thankfulness, toward something beyond the self for the beauty of existence—an awareness of life as a sacred gift from beyond, a clear impression that this we did not and could not do ourselves, and we stand in awe that there is something rather than nothing. In this our heart and mind reach out to God the Creator in grateful appreciation.

Scientific theories of the origins of the universe must assume that random events plus chance account for *why* there is a universe rather than no universe, why there is something rather than nothing. The same is true for theories of the origins of life on this planet. We cannot, and would not want to, return to a cosmology in which the earth was the center of the universe and the universe existed primarily for the benefit of the human race. Random events plus chance may indeed be the best way to understand why we are here in scientific terms. But our ascribing the attribute of Creator to God expresses our strongly spiritual suspicion that in this case, the dice was loaded.[2]

Historical purpose embraces not only a sense of being rooted in a meaningful past, but also a sense of direction for the future. Because the concept of God emerges directly from a quest for meaning, it follows naturally that another aspect we attribute to God is that of *Sustainer*. We feel the split in our being between the transcending abilities of the mind, soul and spirit and the imperfection and mortality of the physical body. Reflective human beings will thus also at various times experience an intolerable and terrifying sense of the insecurity and suspendedness of life. The logicians' argument that just because the sun has risen every morning up till now is no proof it will rise tomorrow may strike many of us as ivory tower nonsense. Yet daily events constantly conspire to force confrontation with the absolute fragility and un-predictability of life, that break through our self-protective barri-ers of psychological denial. If once people were immune to news from outside their relatively small environment, and thus expe-rienced life's tragedies in psychologically more limited and man-ageable doses, people in modern societies are barraged from all over the world with a constant daily diet of natural disasters, ter-rorist attacks, random fatal accidents and crimes. Who among us has not felt the shock of loss and has been thrown back upon questions of ultimate concern by the tragic death of a loved one or some other stark reminder of the frailty of our very lives?

We rebel at the fragility of our lives, our relationships, our emotions, our existence. Where can we turn to make sense of things, to find meaning, in these times of deep despair?

Reflective people seek to understand the material causes of human suffering and despair. We bravely attempt, for example, through such avenues as medical research, to minimize the tragedies that imperil life on this earth. That many of our most gifted people, consistently in generation after generation, devote themselves to this type of research and care for those in need is clear evidence of the vital importance we place in ensuring that human life be sustained.

Yet the sense of existential anxiety that sudden tragedy pro-vokes cannot be comforted fully by the heroic efforts we make to minimize human suffering. It is comforting to know, for exam-ple, that fewer people will die of cancer in the future. But the tragedy of *particular* cases of suffering, those right in front of my eyes, struggling to suck down one more breath of life, is not less-ened by that knowledge. The human soul and spirit senses the inestimable worth of each person and continues to pose the ques-tion, "What about *this* person, my parent, sibling, friend, lover, patient, suffering and dying? How can I make sense of *that*?" It is here that a qualitatively different answer is needed than can be supplied by our heroic efforts to minimize human tragedy. Only submission in the knowledge that through the love of our sus-taining God "all things work together for good" can our griev-ing soul and spirit find comfort in such times of despair.

This is neither the Pollyanna blindness of this as the best of all possible worlds, nor abandoning all to random and imper-sonal fate. Our turn here toward God the Sustainer is a cry of the human soul and spirit that, in the full face of the tragedy of life, we have found, and will again, find meaning and purpose in the universe, in our mother the earth, in human community, and in our individual lives.

* * *

We live at the close of what has been called the modern era. For many generations now, human consciousness has been characterized by a strong separation or distinction between the human sphere and the sphere of nature. In earlier times, it would have been very difficult for any human being to conceive of himself or herself as completely distinct from the order of nature and to view the natural order in purely instrumental terms. The modern consciousness of historicism and individualism, which made possible the development of the capitalist mode of production and was in turn furthered by that mode of production, created an environment in which consumption-wealth was fabricated at a level never before seen in human history. In no previous time did human beings understand or even dream of the material abundance we have found available to us, hidden in the processes of nature. By harnessing nature's power and exploiting nature's raw materials, modern societies have made available to even middle class members a level of wealth once thought reserved only for the gods themselves.

This mode of producing wealth has had its own side effects, however, not the least being a radical alteration of human consciousness itself.[3] It tore apart completely the connection human beings once felt with nature and imposed upon nature a standard of value created by the capitalist mode of production. In modern society, a majestic giant redwood tree, thousands of years old, would henceforth not be seen as an awesome creation of nature to be appreciated and contemplated. It would be seen as containing so many board-feet of building material. Chop it down, saw it up and sell it. (We call this "development.") All values in modern society tend to become instrumental values, reducible to a statistical, preferably monetary, figure on a ledger sheet. Any resistance to such valuation, any sphere of life one hopes to protect from such calculations, is scorned as residual sentimentalism.[4]

We are presently in a transitional phase between modern and postmodern consciousness. The capitalist mode of production, which formed the foundation for the modern consciousness, both contained and aggravated social stratification in the distribution of labor and wealth. Justification for social stratification was found in the doctrine of private property. Property rights and the right to accumulate more property have been an unquestioned value in modern society. Our society takes for granted, as akin to sacred rite, that such accumulation is justified. Many of the values of modern society are positive and are rightly held with high regard. The demystification of nature, allowing scientific investigation and discovery, and the value and rights of the individual, are the most obvious of these.

On the other hand an increasing number of people are realizing that the values thrust upon us by the capitalist mode of production comes at a very high cost. Individual self-interest is pursued even at the risk of destroying the fabric of our social ecology. Communal environments are plundered by "developers" on the one hand and economic dislocation on the other. What is left is pillaged by capitalistic pornographers and drug-pushers.

From strictly within the values of modern society, it is difficult to criticize this environmental destruction. It is an unintended side effect of individual and corporate pursuit of wealth and property. Yet we know intuitively that it is very wrong. This growing awareness of the gap between what is morally right and legally acceptable is a signal of the transitional phase of social consciousness in which we live. Increasingly, groups of people, and even now some of our lawmakers, are recognizing that many of the values of modern society are stagnant. People are beginning to see that distinctions must be made between holding individual rights in high esteem and giving blanket license to unrestrained egoism. New frames of reference are slowly emerging in which such distinctions can be made.[5]

Faced with these problems, many people long for the good old days, a supposed time when order and neighborliness were taken for granted. And indeed, in constructing newer frames of reference we need to draw on both modern and premodern sources of inspiration. It is highly questionable, however, if the current popular nostalgia is socially viable, whether these good old days ever actually existed. Certainly they did not resemble the ideal state in which they are now presented. But this nostalgia for an idealized past does signal our awareness that the values thrust upon us by the modern era are not unambiguous. It repeats a pattern, a recurring theme in all religion, literature and tradition, that the present is fallen or degenerate, compared to a more glorious past.[6]

We do appreciate the demystification of nature and the championing of individual human rights. At the same time, a modern consciousness that views all things, now including even intimate human relationships, strictly in instrumental terms, finally places us at war with each other and at war with the natural order that sustains us. This is clearly destructive of the human quest for meaning and wholeness, despite the greatly enhanced living standard and level of consumption it produced. As we move into a postmodern era, we again find renewed meaning in the concept of God as *Unifier*. God the Unifier is that cosmic voice calling us into supra-individual community with each other and with the natural order. The Unifier God is the embodying source of our own urge to seek unity beyond the egotistical individualism of the modernist ethic.

This is neither an animistic/pantheistic remystification of nature nor a regressive subsuming of the individual into the tribe. It is the profound unity of love, a reflection of the human desire for creative transcendence over and beyond modernity, a modernity so presciently described by Karl Marx and Friedrich Engels in their *Communist Manifesto* as drowning all of our highest moral values and sensitivities in "the icy waters of egotistical calculation." It reflects our growing awareness that modern values, which set us against each other and against the order of nature, are stagnant and in need of fundamental criticism. If these values were progressive and helpful in one period of our history, they now have become regressive and destructive to our quest for meaning, wholeness and purpose. In our renewed attention to the attribute of Unifier in our concept of God, we give expression to that which we feel in the depths of our being, that despite the instrumental values thrust upon us by the modern ethos, we have found, and will again find, meaning and purpose in the universe, in our mother the earth, in human community and in our individual lives.

Though the concept of God is articulated differently in different traditions, we find unmistakable unity in these many conceptions, in that God is posed as a spiritual answer to the human predicament. God reflects the deepest longings of the human soul and spirit. In God we find a more perfect reflection of the creativity, transcending personality and love that is the fruit of the human soul and spirit. In God the human soul and spirit find strength to move forward in love, even in the full face of human tragedy.

But just as creativity, transcendence and love are the natural fruit of the human soul and spirit, these fruits become perverted for those choosing the path of mortality denial. Along this path, the person is drawn primarily to symbols of immortality based on coercive power. Then the image of God, a reflection of the soul and spirit, suffers the same perversions. For those following the path of denial, the analogical imagination produces a God concept based on extrapolations from the hierarchical structures of power. God is seen as the judges' judge, the warriors' warrior, the kings' king, the tyrants' tyrant, the apex of the pyramid of coercive power. God is conceived as an omnipotent ruler who lords it over even the lords and princes of the earth. God becomes that terrible Being seeking to punish, satisfied only with Godself, whose love is unloving and whose justice is unforgiving. Obey this God or else!

This God can be nothing other than mutually supportive of an oppressive status quo. This God is the special preserve of the powerful, the rulers and kings, a God who places the divine stamp of approval on whatever actions bully nations of this world perceive to be in their own selfish interest. This is the God of nationalism, the God who is on *our* side in any and all conflicts, a God for whom reflective self-criticism would be impossible.

It is impossible in the final analysis to establish a loving relationship with such a God. Fear and servitude are the only possible attitude. Ultimately, while giving us illusions of power and direction, this God is defeating of the human quest for purpose and meaning. For a God who acts capriciously, unlovingly, unforgivingly, is no different from that blindness which sees this as the best of all possible worlds—for those who benefit from the present systems of oppression, who say, "How can this be wrong? Your oppression is an illusion, we are really your benefactors, it is God's will that it be so. . . . " It is no different from the bland posture of abandoning all things to random and impersonal Fate—for the rest of us, who say, "My oppression is my own fault, I must deserve it, I am less like God than the rulers, rewards will come in the next life, it is God's will that it be so. . . . "

Human values arise in the context of particular historical circumstances. Values, mores, restrictions, and taboos have specific survival value in specific circumstances. As circumstances change, so must the values of a community change. If values stagnate and the community holds tenaciously to those stagnant values, the people may perish. It is likewise with our conceptions of God. Our conceptions of God reflect the deepest longings of the human soul and spirit. Images of God, conceptions of God, like human values, arise in the context of specific historical circumstances. Our image of God sets the parameters of human response to our circumstances. Thus a stagnant conception of God, like a stagnant value system, may produce tragic results.

Those walking the path of acceptance are best able to perceive the need for new formulations of community values because they regard present community values as tentative. They view present community values as opportunities and tools for creation of environments of freedom within which the creative, transcending and loving works of the human soul and spirit may prosper. Because these values are held to be a means to a different end, it is possible to notice when these values hinder rather than foster achievement of that end.

Those following the path of denial are least able to perceive the need for new formulations of community values because they regard present community values as absolute, as ends in themselves. Their entire immortality project is inextricably bound to an insistence that the status quo must, at all costs, be maintained. Because these values are held as absolute, it is impossible to notice if such values are tending to hinder rather than foster the creative, transcending, and loving works of the soul and spirit. When present values are held as absolute, anything that suggests otherwise is considered only as a potentially subversive threat. When the creative, transcending, and loving soul and spirit begin to contravene the utopia of the status quo, the only apprehension of the situation possible is that it is chaotic, wicked, anarchist, blasphemous. To admit any other possibility threatens psychological death, a breakdown of precarious defenses against overwhelming mortality anxiety, to those who follow the path of denial.

So it is also with our conceptions of God. Those walking the path of acceptance are best able to perceive the need for new models of God because they hold present models to be tentative, a means to a different end. They experience freedom and mutuality in relation to any particular model of God. They view present images of God as tools for building environments of freedom within which the creative, transcending and loving works of the human soul and spirit may prosper. Because these models of God are held to be a means to a different end, it is possible to notice when these conceptions hinder rather than foster achievement of that end.

Following the path of denial, there can be only servility and obsequiousness in relation to models of God as dominant. The image is held to be static, absolute, an end in itself, beyond the challenge of the human soul and spirit. Those on this path are least able to perceive the need for new formulations of God because they hold one particular construct as absolute, universal, an end in itself. Their entire immortality project is inextricably bound to an insistence that the status quo must at all costs be maintained. So long as any one model is held as absolute, it is impossible to notice if it is tending to hinder rather than foster the creative, transcending, and loving works of the soul and spirit. When one model is held as absolute, anything suggesting otherwise is a potentially subversive threat. When the creative, transcending, and loving soul and spirit contravene the utopia of the status quo, the only apprehension of the situation possible is that it is chaotic, wicked, anarchist, blasphemous. To admit any other possibility would quite literally mean psychological death, a breakdown of precarious defenses against overwhelming mortality anxiety, to those who follow the path of denial.

* * *

At this point in our religious reflections, the inner skeptic begins to pose very real questions. Is God, after all, nothing but a human concept? What about Godself? Does *God exist* or not? Our inner skeptic finally throws down the gauntlet, saying, "Look, if God exists, then God must exist quite apart from human conceptions of God. Is there clear evidence, beyond human feelings and inner urges, for the existence of God?"

This is a question for which there may be no direct answer. Apparently, if God does exist, God has chosen, in the full and positive acceptance of human limitations, to tend the doors of divine perception by a positive sense of faith. If God's existence were clearly demonstrable by hard evidence, faith would be unnecessary. We can, however, make a few observations that may at least help us to live at some peace with our inner skeptic.

First, for both the one walking the path of acceptance and the one following the path of denial, God reflects the deepest longing of the soul and spirit. God is a symbol of immortality. God is a human projection of perfection, the human soul and spirit's insistence that, even in the full face of the tragedy of existence, meaning and purpose can be found. God is our assurance, in the face of despair, that our quest for meaning, wholeness, and purpose has a transcendent source and is itself meaningful. This is circular reasoning, to be sure, as every probing of ultimate concern must be. We have no perch outside of human existence from which to observe and criticize what is going on here. This predicament is one aspect of what we positively accept when we accept ourselves as mortal and finite beings.

Secondly, our inner skeptic's demand for evidence is itself based on the particular mode of consciousness that flowered in modernity. It has become part of what Antonio Gramsci referred to as the "hegemony of common sense."[7] Gramsci pointed out that this hegemony also is a ruling-class preserve and open to criticism. Religious skepticism no less than credulity can serve the purpose of maintaining an oppressive status quo. Just as our conceptions of God set parameters for human response in particular situations, so too does atheism. Therefore, in particular social situations, taking a position for or against the existence of God is an attempt to elicit certain social and political responses. A discussion of the existence of God does not take place in an intellectual vacuum, regardless of how skillfully professional philosophers try to hide their external influences. We have no tools for making anything but tentative pronouncements about the existence of God one way or another.

However, the social and political consequences of a position for or against God's existence in particular situations can and must be examined in the context of those particular circumstances and judged on the basis of the political response each position elicits in those particular circumstances. In short, since no one denies that human beings do have objects of ultimate concern, it is always in each particular circumstance, not in some imagined space of intellectual void, that any discussion occurs; a discussion not of Godself, but rather of *which* god(s) do(es) or do(es) not exist.

Thirdly, whether or not one accepts the word *God* in the context of the deepest longings of the human soul and spirit, all reflective people continue throughout their lives to search for answers to perennial questions of ultimate concern. An open but hard-nosed skepticism is always in order. This skepticism helps us to hold any particular model of God as tentative. But atheism or agnosticism do not automatically lead to or follow from either the path of acceptance or denial. Rejection of belief in God too often leads only to treating as absolute some other human institution, such as the state, the party, an ideology, wealth, power. Without allegiance to anything higher than Machiavellian human power, how does one hold such absolutes as tentative? There is no forward movement in terms of our quest for meaning, wholeness, and purpose, if belief in God is debunked, only to have the void filled by entities even more clearly human in origin. The free and open person would do better to reserve final allegiance for that which is the highest creative conception of the human soul and spirit than to that which is less than the highest.

Finally, it has to be stressed that God is not a simple object, like a table or a chair, or even an energy field. We cannot expect to find evidence for the existence of God by methods honed for discerning the existence of mundane objects. A pragmatic and empirical approach to this question suggests that God's existence in the human realm is inextricably linked to the way people live. A particular conception or model of God is not true because it accurately describes an object to which it corresponds. The truth of any particular model of God is found only in the fact that it sets desirable parameters for human response in particular situations that foster creation of environments of inclusiveness and freedom within which the creative, transcending, and loving works of the human soul and spirit prosper.

* * *

We have, as critical thinkers, learned to be cautious in evaluating evidence presented on a subject in which the one presenting has strong personal interests. Concerning the problem of God, this includes all of us. Undeniably, the very idea of God is projective wish fulfillment. We can take some comfort in the knowledge that sometimes human desires and hopes also correspond to reality. Just because we would like it to be so doesn't necessarily make it *not* so. We could simply ascribe *existence* as an attribute of God, as was done by Anselm and the ontological tradition. There has recently been a marked revival of interest among specialists in philosophy of religion in this line of reasoning. But finally, ascribing existence as an attribute of God doesn't make it so either. Our reason can only leave us with an open question on this point. Belief is possible, but can be explained only on the basis of circular reasoning.[8]

We simply cannot know God, or at least cannot communicate this knowledge to anyone else and thus make it communally available, in any way that bypasses human perception. We are inextricably bound within the nexus of our human limitations for expressing and assessing our images, conceptions and models of God. Whatever God is, our models of God are human conceptions, subject to the varieties of human historical and social existence. Recognizing this, we can then become more socially and politically responsible for our theological constructions.[9] This allows us to become freer and more creative in how we conceive of and present our understandings of God, as well as more dialogically open to encountering other people's conceptions of the divine.

Again in our religious reflections, the inner skeptic raises his accusing head. Does this approach finally mire us in absolute relativism? If all of our concepts of God are human constructs, how can one be any better than another? Have we set ourselves afloat on a sea of relativism without an anchor? Do we not here catch the strong whiff of nihilism as the only realistic understanding of our situation?

Actually, I think this understanding leads us out of the mire of skeptical relativism, which was created in the first place by the collapse of plausibility in traditional, descriptive conceptions of religious language. As a symbol of immortality, different models of God function in different ways, setting different parameters for human response in particular situations.

There are conceptions of God that foster the creative, transcending and loving works of the soul and spirit. Our great teachers in many traditions universally point us toward this by encouraging us to seek God within ourselves, not in the fire and storm but in the still, small voice of conscience, in moments of quiet solitude, to seek God in the creativity, transcendence and love, which is the fruit of the spirit. To know this God, to know thyself, to know the Law written on our hearts, recognizing that the kingdom of God already among us, is to know truly the God, by whatever name, who fosters the inclusive freedom of the human soul and spirit and gives us confidence to act, even in the full face of human tragedy, according to the soul and spirit's creative, transcending and loving promptings.

There are also conceptions of God that stifle the inclusive freedom of the soul and spirit, that produce an atmosphere of fear, doubt about one's own worthiness, mistrust, servility and abasement. Such images of God are the manipulative tools of those who represent the principalities and powers of oppression in this world.

Here believer and skeptic join in solidarity in an attitude of atheism toward such models of God. Far from nihilism, this contextual realization places moral responsibility directly on us for the conceptions of God we choose. We are responsible for promoting models of God that foster the works of the soul and spirit, and for debunking those models of God that pervert the works of the soul and spirit. Just as it is now in our hands to write the next chapter of the human story, just as we can no longer perceive ourselves as passive victims of the Gods or of the evolutionary process, so it is that our conception of God has become functioning, moral/eschatological Omega Point and we must choose the God we will serve.

The biblical God long ago placed just this choice between freedom and servitude squarely in front of us. This is a God whose very name is *I am who I am—I will be who I will be*, and (*nota bene!*) I am *not* who the powerful, the oppressors, those who control the hegemony of common sense, say that I am. This is God, the Creator, Sustainer and Unifier, who stands with the oppressed against the utopia of the status quo. This is God, adopted by a peculiar ancient people, a federal union of rebellious peasants and runaway slaves. This is God, who, through those people, placed this choice squarely in front of each one of us. "Choose this day whom you will serve!"

No, all images of God are not equal. We must apply a functional social and political hermeneutic in accepting or rejecting a particular model of God. *Whose interests* are supported by a particular construct of God? *Whose truth* do we confront there? Our preference for some conceptions of God over others, our inclusion in our model of God some attributes while others are rejected, is finally a communal and personal statement of commitment about where we stand in the ongoing struggle between inclusive freedom and exclusive servitude. In this context, the much discussed "preferential option for the poor" in liberation theology has a very direct and critical consequence for religious reflection. It makes explicit an intuition that it is among the victims of unjust economic structures, of sexism and racism, of homophobia, that we are most likely to hear the most valid expressions of doubt and dissent, of principled atheism, toward hegemonic models of God that mutually support the interests of an oppressive status quo.

Finally, paradoxically, it is our explicit awareness that models of God are human conceptions that preserve us from idolatry. God represents our idea of a perfect being. Therefore, while we construct models of God, awareness of this process itself reminds us forcefully that *we are not God.* Therefore, even for a community fully conscious of its own constructive role in creating and selecting models of God, it is always pure idolatry ever to assume that we and we alone speak or act in God's name, as if our will and the Will of God were synonymous. Likewise, because we are not God, we are not God equally. As human beings, each one of us stands in a state of equality before God. The image of God functions as a powerful leveling idea. It stands as an opposing force to any human pretension that some are more equal than others in the sight of God.

Here we have probed some of the implications of the concept of God as fully incarnate in human history. This brings Christians into direct encounter with that carpenter's son of Nazareth, on whom the Christian faith tradition focuses as a particular, paradigmatic instance of this concept of divine incarnation.

Excursive Update—The danger of all theology (literally: words about God) is idolatry, of mistaking that which is not God for God. One might do well, as the mystics say, to meet God with silence rather than more words! Yet this does not seem humanly possible, and perhaps for good reason. Much recent investigation in cognitive processes points clearly toward a picture of the human mind as containing an unavoidable yearning for satisfying interpretation. This has led at least one leading and highly respected researcher, Michael Gazzaniga, to posit what he terms the "Left Brain Interpreter" that will continue, even on a completely unconscious level, to create narratives of connection and sense between events and experiences, even where, in experimental settings, conditions have been purposely controlled to make sure that no such connections exist.[10]

Because human beings think abstractly, we cannot avoid pursuing satisfying answers to questions of existential and cosmic nature: From where did we come? What is our purpose? Who is in control? Why is there something rather than nothing? We might say that recent research in cognitive science has given empirical, scientific grounding for the quip attributed to Voltaire, that if God did not exist, it would be necessary to invent God. At the same time, even a cursory glance at the history of religions or the psychology of religion makes assent unavoidable to the rejoinder, that if God created humans in God's own image, we have certainly returned the favor.

Our analysis, based on Ernest Becker's theory of generative death anxiety, has shown that the dominant, culturally available conceptions of God are most likely to be idolatrous conceptions falsely constructed on projected models of coercive social power. I reiterate here that we need to understand fully that the inclusive, preferential option for the poor among the body of believers (including the "poor in spirit," those who suffer exclusion and debasement, those who cannot see themselves in the preferred images of God privileged in the dominant religious ideologies—women, racial minorities, sexual minorities, the physically impaired, among others) is not some form of gracious charity proffered for the sake of the poor. Commitment to be inclusive of the poor above all else is the best shot we of the dominant majority have of recognizing and criticizing on an ongoing basis our own idolatry, our own comfort in the consumption of God concepts created in our own image.

4

THE EXAMPLE OF JESUS

Critical reflection on the nature of human thought, language and reasoning processes brings us to recognize that all of human existence occurs within intricate webs of historical particularity. This realization is both frightening and liberating. It is frightening because we know just how weak, how naked, how ill-prepared we are to face up to the radical responsibility this places on our shoulders.

There can be no expectations of aid by *deux ex machina* to step in and remedy our situation if we fail to act responsibly. Our mother the earth is a generous provider, benignly tolerant and forgiving of our species' follies and foibles. Yet she yields her fruits only if we respect and work within her natural order. If in greed we violate that natural order, the earth will cease to be a friendly environment within which to prosper. Forests saturated with acid rain die and cease their alchemical transformation of carbon dioxide into breathable oxygen. A significantly polluted environment will remain uninhabitable, unable further to accommodate our species, no matter how much we might later regret our avarice and recklessness. Eroded top soil in our farmland will not soon be replaced. An environment spoiled by nuclear waste, war or accident will not soon be reclaimed for humankind.

As far as we can tell, the universe will be totally indifferent to our fate if we persist in spoiling the natural environment—our demise would likely benefit some other species, and our mother the earth will then give that species the same shot at flourishing we have been given. There can be no expectation of a cosmic force to stay the hand of humankind should we decide to commit collective suicide. We alone write the future chapters of our collective story. That is truly a frightening realization.

But this realization is also liberating. For it removes us once and for all from the status of passive victims of forces over which we have no control. We can, if we will, create a positive and meaningful future for our race. There is nothing keeping us from this other than the perversions of truth in our own collective soul. Furthermore, we have within us, as close as our skin, the very resources we need to choose that positive and meaningful future. The creative, transcending, and loving prodding of the human soul and spirit is ours to employ if we can still the raging whirlwind within our breast long enough to heed the voice of Torah written on our hearts.[1] We recognize now no less than before that the human struggle is finally spiritual warfare. What separates us from earlier centuries is not their perception of the battle as spiritual and our perception of the battle as something else.

What separates us from them is our recognition that the spiritual warfare is not between reified cosmic forces of good and evil that allowed a human escape from responsibility in the posture of passive victim between these forces. Rather, we know that the spiritual warfare rages primarily within ourselves. We decide the outcome and must accept both the responsibility and the consequences of our choices.

We no longer see God as *out there*, dispassionately viewing the cosmic panorama. Such a God has obviously withdrawn from the scene. The only God with saving power for the human predicament is that God whose image functions in our lives to foster environments of trust and inclusive freedom within which the creative, transcending and loving works of the human soul and spirit are encouraged and may prosper. This conception of God springs forth in response to particular conditions of human concern and is, therefore, fully incarnate in human history. This is the God Who Acts in human history, as a consequence of our actions, our choices, our willingness to seek and act upon the creative, transcending and loving prodding of the human soul and spirit.

This understanding of God, fully incarnate in human history, inexorably leads the Christian back to contemplation of Jesus Christ, the Nazareth carpenter's son, through whom the Christian tradition has applied the symbol of incarnation in a uniquely paradigmatic manner. In the context of God's full incarnation in human history, how may this carpenter's son encounter us today?

* * *

Jesus of Nazareth was born into a worker's family of Palestine, a land suffering under the yoke of Roman military occupation. The traditions surrounding his birth quite intentionally picture this Jesus, this one whom many would proclaim as God's Messiah, God's Anointed, as not being born into the circles of prestige and power in that society. There is nothing about the circumstances of the birth that would lead us to expect great things of this child. God, in anointing this child as a chosen vessel, was once again confounding the hegemony of the status quo.[2]

This confounding of an oppressive status quo has a long history in that peculiar people among whom Jesus was born. The history of this people is presented in narrative forms that repeatedly and explicitly illustrate the contrasts between the path of acceptance and the perversions of the path of denial.

Sociological research into origins of this peculiar people, the ancient Hebrew nation, indicates it emerged from a federal union of two main groups.[3] One of these was a loosely constructed alliance of peasants and mercenary soldiers in Palestine who were in rebellion against the feudal oppression of the city states in the region. Like the city dwellers, these peasants worshipped the god El. The other main group was made up of former slaves who fled from Egypt into Palestine. These runaway slaves, holding to traditions of Mosaic leadership, worshipped the god Yahweh.

The union of these two groups was made possible by the fact that each recognized in the other the common characteristic of rebellion against an established authority of political hierarchy.[4] It was fundamental to the historical experience of both groups that the system of kingship meant, for them, only oppression. Their union into one people was founded on an explicit intention, sealed by the institution of covenant, that among themselves there would be no such authoritarian political office to lord it over the rest of the society. The alternative they developed to the system of oriental kingship was a clan-based tribal federation in which united national policy was subject to the voluntary compliance of the tribes.[5]

The tribes united under a religious cult administered by one of the tribes, who for were kept landless to guard against the simultaneous accumulation of property wealth and religious authority in the hands of one tribe. Because of the diverse cultural background of these people, the bonds of cooperation were not easily developed and had to be continually reaffirmed. Their vision of a society free from the oppression of political tyranny moved them forward. The function of the religious cult was as a mechanism of that affirmation of unity and cooperation.

The god of this religious cult contained elements from the religious traditions these two groups brought with them from before the formation of the federal union. A new conception of God was formed from these diverse traditions, the image of the Lord God (Yahweh Elohim). This God was was seen as generating a morality favoring the weak. Most important, the kingship of this God was not to be mediated by a human despot. The unmediated kingship of God was truly an innovation in the people's religious development and stood as a buffer against tendencies to forget the original social vision and appoint a human king. The majestic power of this God was experienced among these people not through, and therefore analogous to, the structures of political hierarchy, but in the immediate experience of equality, mutual aid and cooperation among themselves.

Eventually this people did forget the social vision that had empowered and helped their original union. After some generations of living in the clan-based tribal federation, the demand for a human king did arise among them. A human king was indeed appointed, yet even in the texts reciting the history of this decision (which were edited in the king's court!) strong indications remain that suggest this was a fundamentally wrong or certainly very problematic decision.[6] The image of God as the God who exalts the lowly and throws down the powerful remained with the people in the message of their prophets and constantly undermined and relativized the pretensions of the king and his ruling class to absolute power.

Hierarchical kingship proved to be a total disaster. Within a very short time it destroyed the unity of the people, with the nation splitting into two separate political entities, a kingdom to the North and a kingdom to the South. In this state of disunity they were easy prey for more powerful neighboring nations. First the Northern Kingdom was conquered and sent into exile, where they were eventually lost to history. And finally the Southern Kingdom was also conquered and sent into captivity.

But among the exiles of the Southern Kingdom, a new conception of God emerged that allowed them to survive as a people, despite their exile. Those attributes of God as the God of the weak, opposing the strong, were given renewed emphasis. Furthermore, this God was affirmed as a God whose love and concern, whose care for the people, was independent of their possession of the land.

There had long been inclinations in the religious traditions of the people to ascribe universality to their God, to claim their God as the only true God. These inclinations proved disastrous during the period of kingship because, despite the warnings of prophets, it led to illusions of invincibility, to illusions that this God would provide the divine stamp of approval on whatever the political state perceived as being in its own best interest. These nationalist illusions were dashed by the conquering Assyrian and Babylonian armies.

Now, among a weak and defeated people in exile, the conception of God's universality was reinterpreted in an affirmation that God is God over all the kingdoms of the earth, even as these kingdoms rise and fall. To honor this God as God was a higher allegiance and duty than to honor and serve any of the princes and kings of the earth. Thus the early anti-kingship currents on which the people were founded re-emerged in the period of Southern exile, in a new conception of God. This God relativized and undermined the pretensions to power and grandeur of all the princes and kings of the earth.

This conception of God was built principally on the currents of anti-kingship present from the foundation of the people, on the ancient image of God as having special concern for the weak and powerless against the powerful, preached by the prophets during and after the period of kingship; and on the currents of the universality of God, tempered and reinterpreted in light of the disastrous experience of human kingship. This conception of God allowed the people of the Southern Kingdom to maintain group identity not only in the period of the Babylonian exile, but in subsequent diaspora, as they spread all over the Mediterranean world. This monotheism has remained a central element in exposing and undermining the pretensions to power and glory of the powerful since that time, even into the present.[7]

Central to the expression of this new image of God was the promise that God would one day anoint a servant who would bring in God's true kingdom such that the kingdoms of this earth would be superseded and a new era of God's unmediated kingship would be recognized by all of humankind. This would be for all people a time of freedom from material scarcity and political oppression. Wars would cease and the creative, transcending and loving works of the soul and spirit would prosper.

* * *

Although the meaning of the declaration would later transform radically as it spread throughout the Greco-Roman world, the generative core of the Christian faith is that this promised one who would inaugurate the kingdom of God is none other than the lowly carpenter's son, Jesus of Nazareth. The enduring message of Jesus is the affirmation that the kingdom of God has come, that the time is now to live in that state of freedom and detachment from the mundane symbols of immortality that the path of denial fosters, and to allow the creative, transcending and loving works of the human soul and spirit to prosper. As the ancient Hebrew God placed the choice in front of the people, "Choose this day whom you will serve!" so Jesus placed a choice in front of his contemporaries. The kingdom of God is among you already if you reach out, grasp it, and live accordingly!

The radical nature of Jesus' message is clearly seen in his attitude toward those mundane symbols of immortality current among his people. One of these was the perennial symbol of wealth accumulation. Wealth accumulation has always had a daemonic lure for human beings. Throughout much of the history of our species, survival has been a very real struggle against scarcity. Material prosperity, therefore, is easily transformed into a symbol indicating more of the life force. Accumulation of wealth becomes a symbol of immortality, a denial of death (scarcity), because it carries the psychic signification of accumulating more of the life force.

Jesus spoke harshly to those who pursued accumulation of more than was needed to ensure survival.[8] Drawing on a conception of God as a God of justice and the provider for all, as having a moral attitude of partisanship toward the poor and the oppressed, Jesus insisted over and again that accumulation of more than is needed to survive is in fact to steal from and exploit those who do not have enough to survive. Wealth accumulation (making it and holding onto it!) stands directly between the rich and their participation in the kingdom of God. In Jesus' view, pursuit of wealth accumulation perverts almost without exception the creative, transcending and loving works of the soul and spirit. It destroys communion between people and assigns a kind of quantifiable, monetary value even to those aspects of human relationships most precious to the spirit.

Jesus encouraged us to give and give generously, out of the creative, transcending, and loving abundance of a soul and spirit in communion with God. Such generous giving does not think of what returns will come from the gift, as if the decision to give or not to give were determined by a cost/benefit analysis on a balance sheet. It is reported repeatedly that among those wealthy people who did understand and follow as disciples of Jesus, their first act was always to give generously to the poor.

Jesus certainly recognized that maintenance of the physical body is a prerequisite to allowing the creative, transcending and loving works of the soul and spirit to prosper. Just as the pursuit of wealth accumulation as an immortality project results in perversion of the works of the soul and spirit, so can the fanatical pursuit of asceticism pervert. Jesus and his circle ate and drank and enjoyed the pleasures of material abundance. Their reaction to the perversions of wealth accumulation was not to practice a corollary perversion in the opposite direction. Rather, it is clear from the record that (to the extent he was accused of drunken gluttony!) Jesus enjoyed material abundance, having enough. Yet at the same time he maintained a tentative and detached attitude toward wealth accumulation. He told us to experience satisfaction with what we have. Material abundance does not mean ever more and more, but rather that we have enough.

Consider the sparrows, the lilies of the field, Jesus told us. They have all that they need for each day and do not strive to accumulate more. They have intrinsic beauty without striving to clothe themselves with ever more costly symbols of prosperity. Our mother the earth is a good place to live, a gift of God the Creator, and will yield her fruits plentifully for our survival. If we are content with what we have, sharing with those in need, the earth is a generous and abundant provider.

Because of its ancient clan system and consciousness of being a chosen people, the family and the nation had become for many a symbol of immortality, something providing the illusion of meaning and security while falling far short of God's kingdom.

In this area as well we find Jesus affirming these social institutions, yet holding them to be tentative, a means to a higher end and not an end in itself.

Bearing children, passing life on to the next generation is a universal symbol of immortality. We all understand intuitively the dictum that we live on through our children. As an expression of investment and responsibility for future generations, this is a very positive human emotion.[9] However, the natural desire to procreate as a project of immortality, as a focus for personal meaning in isolation from higher purposes, can easily pervert the creative, transcending and loving works of the soul and spirit.

Our children then become objects, symbolizing virility, fertility, vitality, more life for ourselves. Children come to be seen as having merit only for their use value, something to take care of us in our old age. Children come to be seen only as extensions of our own personality. We expect them to measure up to our expectations and we experience very personal disappointment, for which we compulsively apply the guilt as thickly as possible, if they follow a path different from that which we project for them. We begin to violate their sense of dignity and worth by transforming the responsibility of parenting, of assisting them in the process of socialization, into attempts to meddle and dictate. In the worst case, our children become status symbols for us, signals to the world of our wealth and potency.

The family is a wonderful thing. The love and mutuality, closeness and relationship, between marital partners, siblings, parents, and children, are certainly gifts of the Creator God. Jesus always affirmed this and is portrayed himself as having a special kind of loving regard for children, often going out of his way to interact with them. However, he demonstrated his attitude of detachment toward the family institution by his rather unusual decision not to procreate himself, and instead to seek that kind of familial closeness and relationship with those of his circle, outside the boundaries of biological connection. The love and intimacy among family members is very good. But the example of Jesus shows us that it cannot stop there. The love that characterizes family relations at their best should be extended beyond the biological unit. Furthermore, when his biological family appeared ready to interfere with his pursuit of God's kingdom, imposing their sense of proper socialization upon him, Jesus did not hesitate to rebuke them and even temporarily disown them.

Likewise, Jesus never disowned nor depreciated his status as a Jew. National or ethnic identification might well be a next step in the process of extending familial love and a sense of mutual aid and responsibility beyond the biological unit. It is very positive to have this sense of belonging and identity with a nation or ethnic group. But for those who made this the basis for placing themselves above others in the eyes of God, Jesus reminded them that "God could raise up children of Abraham from these stones!" His willingness to portray in parable a Samaritan in a positive light, in contrast to other characters, as well as his willingness to converse as an equal with the Samaritan woman, indicates that he understood his status in the national or ethnic group as a means to another end and not as an end in itself.

The Hebrew Law is one of the greatest examples we have of a codification of communal values in all of history. This Law, with its strong sense of social justice, mutual social responsibility and mutual social obligation, has been a light to all people in the Western world and beyond. But where specific interpretations of the Law, of compliance with minutiae of prescriptions and proscriptions had become an end in itself, Jesus, Pharisee of love, felt compelled to debunk. This is not to say that Jesus broke the Law, and he certainly did not abolish it. He understood his attitude and actions as a fulfillment of the Law, as interpretation of the Law in light of God's enduring and eternal love for God's creation. In this, Jesus consciously aligned himself with an already well-established direction of interpretation within the Hebrew religion of his day. He approached interpretation of the Law as a means to an end, the inauguration of God's kingdom, rather than as an end in itself.

Jesus respected the Law and its interpretation as an expression of positive communal values. But at the same time he strongly insisted that calcifying certain interpretations of the Law as unimpeachable authority would stifle the environment of inclusive freedom that fosters the creative, transcending and loving works of the soul and spirit. In such cases Jesus was quick to call interpretive attention to the *intent* of the Law, even going so far as to remind his people that "Sabbath was made for the sake of people. People were not made for the sake of the Sabbath."

* * *

A final area in which Jesus confronted the symbols of immortality which pervert the works of the soul and spirit was in his relation to political power.[10] We find this typified in three sorts of encounters. The first of these was with the occupying Romans.

The Roman state represented the most tangible evidence there was in the ancient Mediterranean world that hierarchical political structures provide the sense of permanence and solidity for which the human hearts long. If ever there was a viable immortality symbol embodied in a political empire with which one could identify and melt into in the sense of security of participation in a higher power, this was it. Yet Jesus' attitude toward the Roman state appears to be a curious combination of total disrespect and disregard for the state as an institution and a respect born of love for the individual people who were representatives of the Roman occupation.

Jesus was more than willing to heal the daughter of the Roman centurion and even held up the faith of this centurion as an example to others. Likewise, he advised his followers to go "even yet another mile" for those Roman soldiers who, as the occupying statutes allowed, conscripted people to carry the soldiers' pack for one mile.

But his attitude toward the Roman state itself was something different altogether. He openly satirized the claims of the Roman rulers to be 'benefactors' of the people. He ironically taught that only those whose loyalties were already with the Roman state owed that state anything, while those whose strivings were toward the things of God, toward the creative, transcending, and loving works of the soul and spirit, owed that state nothing at all. In his responses to Pontius Pilatus, the Roman governor, Jesus showed no disrespect for Pilatus as a man, yet he made it very clear that any power Pilatus might feel he held in the encounter over Jesus was an illusion Jesus did not share. We have no record that Jesus, unlike many other Hebrews in different times and places, had to face directly the question of paying homage to the Roman emperor as a god. But we must conclude from what is recorded that he would have rejected this forthrightly.

A second place where Jesus confronted political power was in his encounter with Herod and the Herodians. Herod was typical of a sort of puppet monarch the Roman state would tolerate and endorse in the suzerain nations of the empire. The Herodians represented a sort of politically compromised and fading Jewish aristocracy. These were the people who, among the Jews, had totally sold themselves to the Roman state in exchange for privileges of maintaining certain of the outward trappings of wealth and power. Jesus seems to have had more respect for the Roman occupation than for these people. He sarcastically called Herod a "fox" and showed explicit contempt for these Herodians. However, we must be cautious about inferring too much about Jesus' attitudes toward this group because his interaction with them in the record is minimal and anecdotal. He mainly interacted with his own kind, the common people and Pharisaic teachers.

A final place where Jesus confronted political power was in relating to the Zealot movement.[11] The Zealots were a terrorist force of national liberation. Their goal was to throw out the Roman oppressors and establish a politically independent state of Israel. There are heated scholarly debates as to Jesus' attitude toward the Zealots, and it is certainly beyond my expertise to sort it all out. Coloration by our own attitudes toward national liberation movements in the present makes this even more complex.

The biblical record reflects the biases of the early church on this issue. We know that the indigenous Jewish Christians of Palestine did not participate in the defense of Jerusalem during the uprisings against the Romans in the generation after Jesus, and we may assume this was justified by way of reference to the memory of Jesus' own teaching. On the other hand, given Jesus' general attitude of opposition toward the Roman state, the fact that his circle of closest disciples definitely did include people who are directly identified as Zealots, and the fact that Jesus himself was martyred by crucifixion, a form of punishment the Romans reserved for political rebels, it is impossible to conclude that Jesus held no common ground with the Zealots.

From a modern, secular point of view it is very difficult to understand just exactly what the Zealots were trying to accomplish. With no other weapons than fists, iron wills and the occasional concealed dagger, they took on the power and glory of the entire Roman empire! Did they really think that by ambushing isolated, drunken Roman soldiers in the night they would wear down the will of the Roman occupation? If so, they simply had no conception of the brutal amount of human sacrifice a colossal immortality project like the Roman empire could chew up and spit out in the enhancement of its own power. The more human lives spent in the defense and expansion of the empire, the *more life* that immortality project contained. It literally fed on the spent blood of its citizens and soldiers, slaves, and the people it had conquered.

We begin to understand Zealot actions only in the context of apocalyptic. In this context, Zealots thought that if they could initiate a popular uprising against the Romans, although certainly collective suicide by any objective standard, it would provoke the cosmic forces to intervene on the side of the Hebrews. This made much sense in a Hebrew context, for even in the great traditions of military victories among their people, the Hebrew military leader often began by purposely *weakening* his army, sending many of the volunteers home, rejecting the use of iron chariots, before going out to meet the opposing armies.[12] In this way there could be no pretension but that the victory belonged to God and God alone. Apocalyptic expectations were strong among the social groups with whom Jesus was associated, and there is sound evidence that Jesus himself shared much of this apocalyptic sentiment. On the other hand, Jesus' clear teaching on love for the enemy, his comments on those who would "take the kingdom by force," and the fact that the generation of Christians immediately following Jesus distanced themselves so unambiguously from the subsequent national uprising against the Romans, are all evidence that Jesus did not share the Zealot vision.

Jesus never denied that the kingdom of God he preached was a movement of national liberation. The Roman occupation certainly perceived it to be just that. But was this liberation a goal in itself, an immortality symbol, or would national liberation be a possible byproduct of living the kingdom of God now? What is clear is that Jesus did not see a politically independent state in Palestine as coterminous with the kingdom of God. His concept of the kingdom was that it was of a completely different order from the kingdoms and empires of this world. His kingdom was *not of this world*; it was seen as *already among you and within you*. One cannot but respect those who, with total dedication, stood up against a colossal tyrannical power like the Roman Empire. To see the nakedness of that great immortality project and act to oppose it is itself an astonishing accomplishment. However, if one opposes such a structure in the name of another project that is less than the kingdom of God, the "good" which follows will be short-lived, since new perversions of the work of the soul and spirit will immediately begin to accrue.

As the poet said,

> To fight, perchance to win! Aye, there's the rub!
> For victory brings privilege and prestige
> And the children of the children of the fighters
> Take it all for granted
> And in turn oppress.

Jesus had respect and sympathy for the Zealots. He clearly agreed that God is morally partisan, biased in favor of those oppressed. But he pointed back to the tradition of the unmediated kingship of God, now conceived on the model of a loving parent, as the source for liberation. Despite the oppressors' claims to glory and authority, we have resources within us already to build that environment of inclusive freedom within which the creative, transcending and loving works of the human soul and spirit may prosper. Then we are not so easily provoked to hatred and violence. Rather, we experience an inner prodding to recognize, respect and love the humanity (the image of God) even of the enemy, the oppressor.

This is not simply an urging toward passive acceptance of oppression. Any comfort the oppressor takes in the nonviolence of those oppressed, but filled with this vision of spiritual resistance, is illusionary. This is, rather, a challenge, a calling, for us to tap into that source of dignity and strength that empowers us, as it has also Mahatma Gandhi, Martin Luther King, Eyad El-Sarraj, Ruchama Marton, Nelson Mandela, Abraham Heschel, Michael Lerner, Elias Chacour, Thich Nhat Hanh, the Dalai Lama. As they and other great spiritual teachers have seen, this power enables us to return good for evil, to keep forgiving and loving enemies until they simply cannot continue in the false mode of perception of their immortality project. When violence opposes violence, humankind simply spins its historical wheels. History moves forward, toward a true consummation of the kingdom of God, toward a full consummation of inclusive freedom within which the creative, transcending and loving works of the human soul and spirit may prosper, only when evil is overcome by good.

Here we have offered some reflections on Jesus' attitude toward various cultural symbols of immortality fostered by the path of denial in his particular time and place. In each case, he chose to reject these as projects unworthy of the kingdom of God. His perspective was informed by a conception of God not based on the exacting tyrant mediated through hierarchical structures of power. He rather experienced God as a loving parent, the one closest to us, the one we address as Abba, whose worship bears fruits of creativity, transcendence and love, the works of the human soul and spirit.

To those who follow a path of denial, of serving a life goal that falls short of the kingdom of God—wealth, servility to calcified interpretations of the Law, national chauvinism, subservience to or armed resistance against the Roman state—Jesus had this to say: "You must be born again! *Metanoiete!* Turn around, change your values! Be resocialized! Leave the path of denial and come into the kingdom of freedom! Accept this new conception of God!"

This is the teaching of that carpenter's son to whom Christian faith points as the paradigmatic incarnation of God's Spirit in human history.

Excursive Update—It is baffling that the dogma of the Trinity became so entrenched in Christian religious ideology. But even more baffling is why this dogma remained fundamentally unchallenged by so many (but by no means all!) of the first generation of Anabaptists in the sixteenth century and then continued more or less without question in the Mennonite tradition.

In the first place, it is agreed upon more or less by all parties that this dogma cannot be finally explained in an intellectually coherent fashion.[13] Its very unintelligibility (mystery) is often proffered by its interpreters as a point in favor of the dogma. I, for one, am never quite sure how seriously to take this as a serious point in its favor. Modern proponents of the dogma generally tend to use the trinitarian vocabulary to designate repeated triadic patterns, without much demonstration at all that these reformulations have anything to do with the dogma as it was originally formulated, or even how its original formulation can be extracted from the intellectual environment of Platonic philosophy in which it was firmly entrenched and not be fundamentally altered. Triadic patterns occur in the religious literature of most of the world's religions, without that necessitating any movement away from true monotheism (or limiting divine nature to three-ness, for that matter.) Whatever the original formulations of this dogma, one cannot help but suspicion that this is dogma has become simply a cultural meme, the most mysterious thing about which is its staying power.

Secondly, whatever the meaning of the Trinity in its original formulation,[14] it is unquestionably clear that its elevation to the status of Christian dogma occurred as an imperial fiat of the fourth century, based on Constantine's need to unify the empire. Therefore, one would think that this would have been one of the key dogmas of the church that would have been critically reappraised by the Anabaptists of the sixteenth century. The fact that this dogma, along with other accretions such as the Sunday Sabbath, were so easily accepted by the mainstream of Anabaptists, and were criticized only on the fringes, is strong evidence in my view to suspect that there is a deep and perhaps fatal flaw in the current consensus among Anabaptist historians that the Anabaptists were motivated by a consistent hermeneutic of biblical restorationism.

Current (North American) Mennonite theology seems content to insist on the trinitarian dogma with little exploration of alternatives. Typical in this regard is the (on the whole quite excellent) work of Duane K. Friesen.[15] While admitting that this dogma is an "obscure, speculative, and controversial notion," Friesen goes on to insist that it is "required" for speaking about God in a Christian way; "profoundly relevant" to how we interpret the larger cosmos and culture; and finally "essential" in providing the church with a practical moral vision.[16]

Yet there is not even an attempt made to explore whether God can be spoken about in a Christian way in non-trinitarian language; whether nontrinitarian interpretations of the larger cosmos and culture might be equally profound and relevant; or whether, in fact (by meaningful comparison) there is any truth to the claim that the trinitarian dogma is essential (i.e., sine qua non) in providing the church with a practical moral vision. This latter lapse is particularly noteworthy in light of the recent thoroughgoing argument by theologian and peace activist Jack Nelson-Pallmeyer[17] that it was the process of deifying Jesus into the second person of the Christian Trinity that closely correlated in Christian theology with move away from a conception of God as essentially nonviolent.

J. Denny Weaver likewise assumes the centrality of the trinitarian dogma for Christian theology without further comment.[18] Thomas N. Finger[19] at least mentions the name of Arius in two short footnotes, but betrays no hint that nontrinitarian ideas of any importance or relevance survived the fourth century. James

A. Reimer mentions in passing that nontrinitarian views were circulating among Dutch Mennonites in the seventeenth century, but he fails completely to explore these ideas at all, or even to cite the relevant sources for others to do the follow up investigation.[20] Reviewing this material, it would seem that the inflated rhetoric about this dogma's essential, profoundly relevant and required nature is matched only by a stolid unwillingness among Mennonite theologians to examine or honestly explore any other possibilities.

Despite my personal view that this dogma is needlessly obscure, unintelligible and, in an interfaith context, seriously and pointlessly divisive, it is not my contention here that the Trinity dogma should be rejected by the Mennonite church. However, I would like to place whatever persuasive powers I have behind the suggestion that we recognize and validate the fact that there are other views among us, and that we (Mennonites) would do well to encourage an embrace and exploration of a wider Radical Reformation identity that includes nontrinitarian understandings of the nature of God (as found, for example, among seventeenth century Dutch Mennonites, Seventh Day Adventists, many Quakers and, of course, Unitarians and Unitarian Universalists.)

At the very least, public assent to the trinitarian dogma should never be the prerequisite for Mennonite church membership; Mennonite theologians ought to take special care that current confessions of faith reflect only actual biblical language; that Mennonite theologians, pastors, and teachers seriously educate the Mennonite people in the *political* history of this dogma (about which very few, in my experience, have even a clue); and Mennonite theologians, pastors and teachers should begin the process of exploring and educating Mennonite people in at least those nontrinitarian views that are unquestioningly present within the Anabaptist and Radical Reformation historical stream.

5

TOWARD A
CRITICAL CHRISTOLOGY

Jesus of Nazareth proclaimed to his contemporaries that the kingdom of God is near, that what we need do to enter the kingdom of God is to believe in it and live accordingly. Living according to the kingdom of God meant to forsake those values thrust upon us by the dominating power hierarchies and instead to treasure human community, mutuality and trust. The idols of our immortality projects destroy human community, mutuality, and trust, slowly binding us to systems of domination and oppression. In answer to this human predicament, Jesus, Pharisee of love, preached a conception of God based on the model of a loving parent. In the value system generated by this conception of God, the "least of these" are held in highest esteem. The one who would be the greatest should become the servant of all. The first shall be last and the last shall be first. It was, in short, an ironic reversal of the hierarchical value systems.

Jesus' teachings as we have had them handed down to us are neither systematic nor exhaustive. It is clear that a very large part of the impact he had on his followers had not so much to do with his teachings *per se,* but his teachings in package with his personality, life and example. Around Jesus, many of his followers caught a glimpse of what life in that kingdom of God was like—a kingdom of freedom, where the creative, transcending, and loving works of the soul and spirit are nurtured and prosper. As with our experience today, a central place where that new perception became a reality was eating at table. The resurrection legends of the tradition go so far as to say that two of his circle did not even recognize Jesus until they sat down to eat with him.

Jesus was killed, murdered by the Roman occupation forces. This was a stark reminder to his followers that this new kingdom of freedom would be perceived as a mortal threat to those whose values were formed by the hierarchical systems of oppression. It was a starkly frightening lesson and the tradition says that, at least initially, his circle of followers scattered in fear.

Yet the experience of the kingdom of God, which they had had in their association with Jesus, proved stronger than their fear. Exactly how it happened remains a mystery. Immediate followers of Jesus are said to have witnessed his resurrection from death, but the extant sources reporting this come from decades after the event, and it is unclear even in these sources exactly what is meant by this claim. Some sources seem to indicate the reanimation of an already entombed and decaying corpse. Other sources indicate a spiritual body that could pass through walls. Still other sources (the oldest of those extant) speak more in terms of a heavenly vision. Competent historians continue to disagree on how these sources should be weighed and interpreted. In any case, what is undisputed is that the vision of the kingdom of God these followers caught from Jesus lived on in them after Jesus' death. They regrouped and, now with a renewed fervor of genuine conviction, began to spread the good news of God's kingdom themselves. Because of them, in the words of Willi Marxsen, *"die Sache Jesu geht weiter!"* The cause of Jesus lives on![1]

* * *

Jesus' closest followers, probably following the lead of Simon Peter, began to preach that Jesus, although murdered by the Roman occupation forces, had been raised to new life by God. Jesus, they now taught, had in fact been the promised Messiah, the anointed one, who brought in the kingdom of God. Dying and being raised to new life became a powerful metaphor for the call to become part of the Jesus movement, those who were living the kingdom of God already. These people began to refer to Jesus with honorific titles, such as Lord and King, which Jesus abjured during his own lifetime.[2]

It is now a well-established consensus among scholars that in his preaching, Jesus did not point to himself but rather to God as the proper focus for religious devotion.[3] Yet we find already

in the earliest strata of Christian documents, such as the first epis-
tle of Paul to the church in Thessalonica, a dual focus on both
"God the Father and the Lord Jesus Christ." In other words, from
the earliest times of which we have record, the religion of Jesus
was beginning to be turning into a religion *about* Jesus.[4]

There are parallels to this phenomenon of the messenger becoming the message in the history of religion. The most obvious
example is that of Gautama Buddha, teacher of enlightenment,
who then, as his teachings were developed by later generations
into an identifiably separate religion, became the focus of worship in many forms of that religion, though this clearly contra-
dicted many specific aspects of his teaching itself. In the case of
Jesus and Christianity, we, the heirs of the Christian tradition,
must also try to make sense of this development in our religious
reflection.

Jesus pointed to a conception of God based on the model of
a loving parent. The church increasingly focused on Jesus himself, proclaiming him first as the eschatological Messiah who
would return, then as the Lord and Christ who was already reign-
ing in heaven with God, then eventually as a divine person in the
Godhead. Jesus was deified in the collective development of
Christian ideology.

If we remember that the religious urge is inextricably bound
to the human quest for meaning, we can sympathize with those
who, in stages, deified Jesus. Their own sense of meaning and
purpose could not be separated from their hope for an eschatological redeemer or from the taste of God's kingdom they experienced in communities gathered in the name of Jesus. As they
struggled to express a conception of God that would adequately
reflect the sense of meaning and purpose they had found in gatherings in Jesus' name, it followed that group images of Jesus himself would begin to play an increasingly crucial and central role
in their conception of God. God symbolized their greatest hopes
and the group images of Jesus were the center of those hopes.
Each community of "Jesus people" developed their own ways to
articulate this experience.

Among the earliest Christians, who were Aramaic Jews in
Palestine, Jesus was seen as having been appointed by God as the
apocalyptic Son of man who would finally bring an end to history. Jesus taught what has been called a "present-future" view
of God's kingdom.[5] This was carried on in the table fellowship

of the Aramaic Jews who were followers of Jesus. But already in ascribing the role of the Son of man to Jesus, we see a subtle shift in emphasis occurring, whereby it was possible to distinguish between the present and future in God's kingdom. They taught that Jesus would return in his role of the Danielic Son of man very soon, already in their own lifetime, topple the mighty, and bring an end to human history (cf. Daniel 7:13ff.).

Greek-speaking Jews who were followers of Jesus also taught that Jesus would play the role of the returning apocalyptic Son of man. But they added their own spin, that as the Christ, Jesus already ruled in heaven already during the interim before his return. Here we see a new emphasis pointing toward a divine aspect of Jesus' own nature added to the teaching of the Aramaic community. Finally, as the Jesus movement spilled over into the Gentile world, Gentile converts began to imagine Jesus in purely ontological terms, as the pre-existent Son of God, the Logos, who briefly came to earth and then returned to heaven after his death.

This early Christian transformation in their teachings about Jesus has to be understood in light of the fact that they often found themselves in situations of extremity. As the Roman empire continued its lumbering course of collapse, many of its rulers became increasingly tyrannical and drunk with a decadent sense of their personal invincibility. Many of these rulers demanded that they be worshipped as divine beings themselves. The early Christians often refused this demand. Yet on what basis could they stand up to the Roman Emperor, the most powerful person on earth at that time? The more power and glory the Caesar claimed for himself, the more power and glory the church claimed for Jesus. In short, the claim that "Jesus is Lord!" had as its direct correlative "Caesar is *not* Lord!" With this in mind, we can understand and sympathize with those who deified Jesus ben Joseph of Nazareth. It was not just imaginative mythmaking gone wild. It was a powerful survival strategy.[6]

* * *

Sympathy with the process of the deification of Jesus does not entail uncritical acceptance, however. The fact is, this entire tradition has become problematic for many Christians since at least the seventeenth century. For some 300 years already, at least some thoughtful Christians have been feeling uncomfortable with simplistic acceptance of miracle stories in the Bible, which cast a long shadow of primitive superstition over the narratives. However, during most of this time it was never seriously questioned that there do indeed exist transcendent universals, given by a transcendent God, that can be objectively known, either through reason or revelation. Our post-Enlightenment historical consciousness forces some of us in our time to question this deeply. The entire tradition of an ontological Godman has itself become problematic and has left many of us wondering what, if anything, all of this could possibly mean to us today.

On both intellectual and moral grounds, it seems implausible that we should expect a divinely instigated apocalyptic end to human history (one of our own making is a different story.) We no longer conceive of God as a Being who stands apart from the natural order and intervenes at will in that order. Our quest for a sense of meaning and purpose now takes place in circumstances very different from that of the earlier Christians. We understand that we cannot depend on an apocalyptic Son of man or any other force to step in from outside human history to save us should we continue in our march toward collective suicide. If the metaphor of Christ-as-Divine-incarnation can mean anything at all in our time, it can only point us to the relativity of all of our conceptions of God and emphasize that we are ourselves hold responsibility for our future.

For centuries now, the deified Christ has been the focal religious icon of the powerful social, political and religious institutions of Western culture. Two millennia of history have accumulated that have identified this deified Christ as the symbol of divine sanction for hierarchical systems of oppression, economic exploitation, imperialist conquest, and colonial occupation. These "pyramids of sacrifice," to borrow sociologist Peter Berger's term,[7] must be defended by an adequate sacrificial ideology, and for two millennia the crucified-cum-deified Christ has been the primary sacrificial ideology at the core of Western civilization. As we enter the twenty-first century, serious religious reflection cannot ignore this history and move on as if from scratch.

Inasmuch as the deified Christ has become one more immortality symbol in whose service people are killed, marginalized, and kept in bondage to systems of oppression, we must be willing to let that deified Christ go. We must take a stand of unbelief toward that Christ. Inasmuch as a deified Christ allows us to escape responsibility in a posture of resignation or passivity toward oppression and our march toward collective suicide, we must be willing to let that deified Christ go. We must take a stand of unbelief toward that Christ. Inasmuch as a deified Christ has become a symbol under which to conquer, we must be willing to let that deified Christ go. We must take a stand of unbelief toward that Christ.

Inasmuch as a deified Christ divides us from our brothers and sisters of other religious traditions, we must be willing to let that deified Christ go. We must take a stand of unbelief toward that Christ. Inasmuch as a deified Christ confirms us in our prejudices of race, religion, class, sex and sexual orientation, allowing us to feel righteous in our exclusion from fellowship many people whose lives have been undeniably touched by the love of God, we must be willing to let that deified Christ go. We must take a stand of unbelief toward that Christ.

We have no choice but to be critical of the Christian tradition. Just as we must assume ethical responsibility for our conception of God, so must we also assume ethical responsibility for our teaching about Christ.[8] For Christians, the two are inseparable.

* * *

On what, therefore, might we base a positive Christology, a positive use of the metaphor of Christ-as-Divine-incarnation, for our time? I offer the following points for further exploration.[9]

We know by experience that life is not reducible to either the material or the nonmaterial. We must reject, therefore, any attempt to present ultimate reality, ultimate concern, as either mental or material activity. Any experience of life includes both the material and mental/spiritual aspects. We experience the unity of the material and mental/spiritual aspects of our being most concretely in our relationship to ourselves and other people. Therefore, we can best express our ideas about ultimate reality, ultimate concern, by employing personal metaphors.

This sense of unity is felt most strongly in relationships of love. Love respects the independence of the other as a personality and resists in relation to the loved one those value systems that divide or fragment the loved one. Therefore, as we employ personal metaphors to express our experience of ultimate reality, ultimate concern, we do well to relate those metaphors as closely as possible to the concept of love. In employing personal metaphors closely related to the concept of love to express our experience of ultimate reality, ultimate concern, it is no longer possible to hold nonpersonal institutions, such as, especially, the state, as the locus of highest moral authority. Moral authority springs only from the creative, transcending, and loving promptings of the soul and spirit.

Christians may well find the personal metaphors of the Christological tradition useful and meaningful. If so, we are free to employ them. But we are not compelled to do so. As this relates to Christological language, we may well find that titles such as friend, helper, teacher, and sibling (brother, sister) are better metaphors than those stemming from relations of hierarchy (Lord, Master, King). It may be that for certain terms heavily laden with hierarchical overtones, it would be best to encourage a moratorium on their use for the time being. This is not something to be proscribed by theologians. Theologians must, rather, be attentive to those metaphors that are used and those that are neglected among the least powerful sectors of the community and use that as a guide in their constructive work.[10]

As much as possible we must work to reverse the process of exchanging the religion of Jesus for a religion about Jesus. Jesus pointed toward the direct experience of the kingdom of God in the present-future. It was certainly not his intention that his message of the presence of God's kingdom of freedom should devolve into yet another form of religion. We cannot change the fact that that is what happened. We need not abandon the Christian religion, any more than Jesus abandoned Judaism. It is our religious tradition, and despite its faults has proven power to motivate love and concern among its followers.

Nevertheless, we can see clearly the manner in which the early church shifted the message of Jesus. The church hypostatized the present-future kingdom Jesus proclaimed, identifying it with Jesus himself. By use of first functional and then ontological Christologies, the church reduced the kingdom of God to one man.[11] Jesus invited all of us into God's kingdom of freedom. But once the kingdom became focused on one man, the gate was effectively closed to the rest of us, at least in this life. The promise of heaven in the next life is scant replacement for Jesus' invitation into the kingdom in the present-future. We must reclaim from Christian tradition our invitation to enter that kingdom now.[12]

This process led directly to a second shift the church brought about in the message of Jesus. Jesus focused his attention on the present future, a radically prophetic view of time. But once the church began to focus on Jesus rather than on the kingdom Jesus proclaimed as the locus for meaning and purpose, it was inevitable that his view of time would be replaced with a scheme of salvation history in which Jesus became the "center" of history. [13] In this scheme, the present loses all significance, except as a veil of tears through which one must pass on the way from the *past* salvation worked by Christ to the *future* salvation worked by Christ.

This had a particularly detrimental effect on Christian ethics. For whereas in Jesus' teachings, the promise of eschatology was translated into the demand for spontaneous acts of justice, love and mercy, in the new scheme, only the *works* of the church, those prescribed rituals designed to get us through this insignificant present, could be valued.[13] Jesus' message that the future is already present, that forgiveness, grace, and mercy are everywhere in the liberating practice of love, that God had taken presence in the people, was first obscured and then lost in the Christological formula of a preexistent, incarnate, and then exalted Son of God.

The early Christians assigned titles and offices to Jesus Christ in an attempt to express what it was about this man that was unique, different from other human beings, for them. It was their attempt to express that special quality they experienced when gathered for table fellowship in Jesus' name. Is Jesus still unique for us today? Or to put the question in its traditional form, "Is there salvation outside of Christ? "

This is a hard question to answer because it assumes intimate experience of other religious traditions. It should be referred to those who have such an intimate experience. As far as I understand it, there appears to be a great similarity between Jesus and the Buddha, not only in the fact that both pointed to the freedom of living in the present-future, but also in the way the followers of both magnified their teacher after his death.

Jesus' ethical teachings have parallels in all of the great religious traditions, and all of his teachings can also be found in the rabbinical sources of his contempories.[15] Even his vision of God's kingdom of freedom in the present-future has also been taught by other great religious figures: the Buddha, Francis of Assisi, the Baal Shem Tov, Martin Buber, and many others.

Of course Jesus was unique in the sense that all individuals are unique. Jesus stood in a particular historical communal tradition. Because of this, Jesus was tempted by similar paths of denial which we face today as well—accumulation of wealth, deification of the state, the family, ethnic group and its communal law code. In each of these cases, as was seen, his attitude to these symbols of immorality remains instructive for us today.

On the other hand, no matter what titles and offices of honor we ascribe to Jesus, when we face some of the great ethical questions of our day—biomedical issues, family and sexual issues, the arms race, global economic issues—we simply draw a blank from Jesus' own direct teachings. The most we can find there are some principles, which we must then interpret and apply. But we are most likely to do this completely out of context, and in any case, these are then our interpretations and applications, not those of Jesus.

The point is, no matter how magnificent the language we employ in our Christological doctrines, it is impossible to follow Jesus as some new kind of legalistic code. He simply had nothing directly to say on many of the most pressing issues of our day. We are left to follow our own best prompting of the soul and spirit on these things, whether we picture Jesus as a human prophet who lived and died, or as the pre-existent Son of God who reigns in heaven sitting on the right hand of the Father. And we are more likely to remain humble with our interpretations and applications within the context of the former construct.

What we do have is Jesus' promise that if we "seek first the kingdom of God," that is, if we genuinely listen to the creative, transcending and loving promptings of the soul and spirit and determine as much as possible to live in the present-future of the kingdom of freedom, then "all the rest will be given to you." But again, this promise is made credible not because it was given by an ontological God-man. It is made credible in the actual experience of those who strive to be in tune with the creative, transcending and loving promptings of the soul and spirit.[16]

The question of the uniqueness of Christ has traditionally been expressed in the question, Is there salvation outside of Christ? In our time, as we stand in solidarity with the victims of Christian antisemitism, with our native American brothers and sisters whose genes still carry the effects of smallpox purposely inflicted on them by Christians, with our once enslaved black brothers and sisters, with the victims of economic and cultural imperialism, with people marginalized by sexism, with people condemned and excluded by homophobia, with the victims of Western Christian culture, the question is reversed: Can one still find salvation in Christ?[17] Our Christological reflections cannot escape or ignore this new consciousness. We believe that one can find salvation, meaning and purpose in Christ. But not in those christs who presided over and provided the religious and moral justification for such marginalization and murder.

The entire urgency of the question of the uniqueness of Christ arises only for those who have made some particular Christ into an immortality project of denial. Only then does one perceive as a threat the recognition of the same truth from other sources. Those who have experienced the present-future kingdom of freedom and mutuality at table fellowship with those of other belief systems are not likely to feel much urgency in defending the uniqueness of their Christ.

Nevertheless, for those brought up in the Christian tradition, the God they find in the deepest levels of their soul and spirit will likely continue to wear the face of Christ. What we affirm about Christ is inseparable from what we affirm about God and, ultimately, about our own lives. If grasping that present-future kingdom of love and freedom is still an option for us, fidelity and Christian faith obligates us to reach out for it, even if that means demythologizing and even abandoning entirely pre-existent/incarnate/exalted Christological language. With a nod to the current popular icon *WWJD* (what would Jesus do?) I suggest this is, after all, what Jesus would do.

Excursive Update—Although I changed little in these last two chapters since their first publication, I have come to see that I was probably needlessly confrontational on the Christian claim for the *uniqueness* of Christ and of Christian truth. Furthermore, I actively support the claim of *universal relevance* of Christian truth (understood as the paramount importance of living together in love, even with those with whom we differ, even with "enemies") for all people. On subsequent reflection, I think my antagonism spent there is really directed at claims for the *superiority* of Christian truth (that this truth of how we ought to live is found in twenty-four carat purity only in Christianity); the *exclusivity* of Christian truth (only Christians, in the final analysis, could know the truth because God has only revealed divine truth in the Christian revelation); the *normative nature* of Christian truth (all people responding affirmatively to this truth must eventually leave any other religion they hold behind and convert to Christianity.)

I think one can hold with all integrity convictions about the uniqueness of Christ or Christian truth (it is not found in just this way in any other religion) and universal relevance of Christian truth (all people—including most Christians!—need to hear and respond to the message of the paramount importance of living together in love, up to and including love of enemies). I think we can proceed in mission work with all that entails, such as responding to people's physical, emotional, spiritual needs, and building *demonstration communities* in which this message is exemplified in concrete terms. I think we can do all this, however, without insisting that other faiths are inferior, have at best a tainted avenue into this message, and must be left behind in conversion to Christianity.

In fact, a demonstration community predicated on the implicit or explicit demand that "We will have only one religion here, thank you," will almost by definition not be able to properly demonstrate the power of the gospel message to unify people in love despite their differences. And such a demonstration is needed, given that religious differences are among those historically—and very much still today—the most powerfully able to keep people apart.

Given how many centuries Christians have been insisting on the superiority, exclusivity, and normative nature of the Christian religion, and how entwined this claim has been with corollary claims about Western culture, simple honesty would have us admit it is hard indeed for us at this time to proclaim the uniqueness and universal relevance of Christ and Christian truth without smuggling in assumptions about the superiority, exclusivity, and normative character of Christ and Christian truth as well—often against our own best intentions.

It is these latter claims that for the most part are hardest to let go, because these claims (due to human sin, as seen in chapter two) are most useful in building strong, worldly institutions, including church institutions. This is why it seems so dangerous and anxiety-provoking to think the faith without these claims. Proposing a view that does not assume the superiority, exclusiveness, and normative character of Christianity quickly elicits the objection that this would empty the church pews.

Be that as it may, I do think it would be instructive once in awhile to begin our reflections on the meaning of self-sacrificial love at exactly this point of protecting our religious institutions. What if God's plan of sacrificial love in this world had not to do with individual people converting to one religion so much as providing in history a powerful institution that would willingly be weakened even unto death (going out of existence) in the pursuit of the goal of making this love known in the world? In that light, efforts to insulate and protect the institutions at the expense of accepting institutional vulnerability for the sake of love and interfaith understanding appear quite different.

In this light, among Mennonite approaches to interfaith issues, the dialogical proposal of Dorothy Yoder Nyce[18] is especially important and powerful. This is the case precisely because she offers concrete, well-thought-out, and spiritually grounded exercises for thinking through Christian truth, holding to claims of uniqueness and universal relevance, while consciously criticizing claims of the superiority, exclusivity, and normative character of the Christian religion.

6

CHURCH WITHOUT DOGMA

*T*he church formed and progressed through human history with a strong conviction that God calls it into being and directs it in a special and particular unity. In this light, there is no doubt that the *ecclesia*, the gathered group, will find itself called into unity on a different basis than through a transcendent command. As we move further into becoming a truly *post-Christian* society, unity emerges only as people of faith begin to work out new paradigms for understanding and interpreting their life together. This is an inevitable event in the demise of the Constantinian captivity of the Christian religion, wherein for centuries Christian religious ideology and secular authority acted as mutually reinforcing elements of social control.

Beginning at least in the sixteenth century, the church as an institutional power has been declining. Before the Protestant split, it may have been possible to speak of *the* church, although this also betrays a decidedly Western Eurocentric perspective. In any case, it is impossible to speak that way of the past five hundred years of history. Increasingly, *the* church is a meaningless abstraction.

What we must speak of instead is of many and diverse churches. These churches do not speak or respond in unity on even one of the major social or doctrinal issues of our day. A profile of how these churches do respond to the pressing social issues of our day would likely parallel closely the responses of society generally, reflecting the same attitudes of class and race, despite claims to guidance from transcendent sources.

The function of this claim to transcendent guidance (as reading now with hindsight the nineteenth century Christian discussions of race and slavery makes clear) has been to confirm people in their prejudices, to mask and obscure the social and political sources of these prejudices, and to cut off further discussion of the issues involved. Therefore, an approach to religious reflection that does not assume a transcendent source of guidance, but instead strives to make explicit its social and political vision as the basis for communal gathering of people of faith, does not *create* disunity among the churches. It begins with the social fact of disunity and attempts to reflect religiously within that context, with a firm conviction that a people called together as a *community of demonstration* is a highest divine calling, to exist as living active evidence that human beings of diverse backgrounds and beliefs can, with concern for inclusiveness and social justice, live together in peace, freedom, and mutual respect.

* * *

The churches historically have sought unity on the basis of the language they employ—that is, as a unity of creed and doctrine. In many ancient cultures, but particularly in those cultures out of which the churches arose, speech was seen as a particularly powerful act, and the Word (*logos*) was viewed as supernatural, if not explicitly magical. To name an object gave power over that object, and naming of children was a particularly significant act. It was assumed that the child would acquire traits contained in the name itself. Therefore, it is quite clear why so much stress would be placed in the past on correct verbal formulations of religious truth.

Modern linguistic theories also stress the importance of language in shaping social reality. Although it seems likely that we carry a general and vague prelinguistic experience of reality into adulthood, it is a reality that cannot be articulated outside of language. The power of language does not reside in the words themselves, but in language as an integral component of a complex social and cultural experience that must be learned.

Through language the person learns the social codes that convey the meaning of the social experiences of other people. Through language a person communicates to others his or her own cultural experience and so learns to situate himself or herself in the cultural environment. Learning correct use of language is the most important part of the process of socialization. It is through a common use of language that people communicate.

Therefore, while there may or may not be enduring prelinguistic experiences of reality, the developed communication process does assume prior, common cultural experience. Interlocutors must have learned to use language in compatible ways for the communication process to take place.[1]

The most basic experiences are common to all people. "I am hungry" generally requires no more than literal translation of the words into a tongue common to the interlocutors for communication to take place. As concepts become more abstract, however, literal translations become increasingly unsatisfactory. Dictionaries can easily be programmed into computers. Yet translations of even simple business letters produced by this method of literal translation of words are unintelligible unless closely controlled by one who has command of all languages involved in the translation. This is painfully obvious to anyone who has tried to assemble a child's toy on Christmas morning following enclosed instructions produced by such literal translation!

To learn a foreign language, grammar books are helpful only up to a certain point, beyond which the learner must be immersed in the history and literature of the people who speak the language. One must share in the cultural experience of the people, seeing life the way they do on a level at which the cultural meaning of the words employed are formed.[2]

A common experience of life is necessary for communication between people. Word symbols employed in the communication process in turn shape a person's own experience of life.[3] Language is the tool of a dialogue process between a person's internal and external experience of reality. Therefore, some internal experience of reality is logically before the communication process. Through language, a person tests his or her own experience of reality with that of other people and assimilates other people's experience of reality into his or her own interpretations.

In normal circumstances we take the communication process for granted, for the forward movement of living continues on in stable fashion. Most often, we share a common cultural experience with those with whom we come into contact. Communication in everyday life proceeds at such low levels of abstraction that even newcomers can pick up the necessary background of experience rather quickly. Yet our humor is full of situations in which there is a snag in the communication process. Americans and English people (who, as the quip goes, are divided by a common language) do the same thing in response to the command to "Fasten your safety belts." But they might do quite differing operations in response to the command, "Remove your bonnets."

While such situations cause momentary embarrassment, we have a well-established method for sorting out the difficulty. We point to the object designated by a particular word. So long as *actions* correspond, we are justified in assuming that valid communication has taken place. When our actions do not correspond, we know we must retrace our steps and sort out the difficulty.

* * *

This point is made clear by Anatol Rapoport in his book *Operational Philosophy*.[4] He demonstrates why the language of natural science has been so fruitful. Discourse in the natural sciences has proceeded by way of agreed methods for sorting out snags that occur in communication. This is easiest when there is a concrete object to which one can point. But that is not always the case, even in the natural sciences. In such cases, says Rapoport, scientists must use an "extensional bargain." Agreement that communication has taken place is based on observing common actions among the communicators. The higher the level of abstraction— the further away interlocutors get from objects to which they can point—the more an extensional bargain must be relied upon.

Discussions of such high abstraction were passed off by logical positivism as "non-sense." That kind of strident, anti-clerical atheism is often applauded in academic circles when censuring the metaphysicians of religious thought. But now we have come to see that this same analysis would apply equally to much of the conversations, as one example, of theoretical physicists. At very high levels of abstraction, where we are far away from simple objects toward which to point and where our most vital human conversation takes place, extensional bargains are necessary and unavoidable if valid communication is to proceed.

The categories employed in religious thought are among the most abstract concepts in human language. In religious thought, the conversations with which people attempt to communicate their experience of faith with others, frequent and conscious use of extensional bargains must be expected. Yet this is exactly what is truncated and curtailed when adherence to a creedal or doctrinal statement is the foundational basis for unity among people of faith. Relativism on the level of language, adhering to the doctrines while in fact interpreting the meaning of these doctrines in every possible direction, is relativistic to the core, and yet is the only way religious bodies can possibly hold themselves together on the basis of a common creedal or doctrinal statement.

If genuine communication within the body of freely gathered people of faith is to proceed, we must help a shift in our thinking away from adherence to creedal or doctrinal statements and toward a unity based on demonstrated corresponding actions, a corresponding moral and ethical stance of compassion in the world. A person's moral and ethical stance toward the world is a more accurate indicator of the spiritual life of that person than is the doctrinal language employed by that person to communicate his or her spiritual commitments.[5] A spiritual life of fear and mistrust, of the path of mortality denial, will be made public in actions. A spiritual life of love and trust, of the path of mortality acceptance, will be made public in actions.

A unity based on the doctrinal language employed to communicate spiritual life may or may not constitute a unity of spiritual life among a people of faith. Suppse we assume that a spiritual life of love and trust, of the path of mortality acceptance, will issue in a moral and ethical stance in the world most broadly characterized as pacifistic.[6] And suppose we assume that a spiritual life of fear and mistrust, of the path of mortality denial, will issue in a moral and ethical stance toward the world most broadly characterized as not-pacifist. Then we may see which path is followed as key to perceiving a person's spiritual life.

It is interesting to note that churches unified on a creedal and doctrinal basis have repeatedly been able to maintain their unity only by accepting that they will be divided internally exactly by the issue of the morality of Christian participation in armed conflict. That such an internal division exists and will continue to exist is the official position of these churches. Such churches consider their teachings on active participation in military service to be an accidental, not an essential, of Christian faith. Therefore, if we consider Jesus' teachings on love for the enemy (which minimally must include not participating in the organized destruction of national enemies) to be at the heart of the Christian faith, and not on the periphery of the faith, we must assume creedal or doctrinal unity is not a good indicator of spiritual unity.

A unity among people of faith based on an observable common moral and ethical stance in the world is a more adequate indicator of spiritual unity. To the extent that a unity of the spirit is desirable among the gathered people of faith, we must conclude that a morally and ethically based unity is more desirable than is common consent to a particular creedal, confessional, or doctrinal statement.

* * *

Unity based on a common moral and ethical stance in the world requires frequent and conscious striking of extensional bargains. When agreement is not found on the level of language, we must then proceed on the basis of shared moral and ethical concern, mindful and respectful that each person's way of saying it is one fallible attempt to express in words a common and shared spiritual life.

Word symbols are tools employed to express a person's spiritual experience. These word symbols reciprocally shape the spiritual life of each person. How particular word symbols are assimilated by each person depends on the particularities of cultural context and, within particular cultural contexts, of individual biography. Because individual biographies are subjective and personal, it cannot be assumed that word symbols used to communicate a person's spiritual life will be employed or understood uniformly by everyone, even people within the same cultural environment. The language, metaphors, and symbols chosen by each person may differ significantly from one person to another. But we can respect the integrity of each variant expression because of a deeper common unity, pointing toward a unity of the spirit, which we see on the level of moral and ethical commitments in the world.

Let us illustrate by looking briefly at two people who employ directly contradictory language in relation to the concept of God. One says God exists. The other insists God does not exist. Clearly, on the level of language, there is no common ground here. But division does not occur because each continues to assume a spiritual unity, recognizing in the other a common moral and ethical stance in the world. Each sees that the other encounters the world in terms of trust and love. Recognizing this in the other, a mutually respectful extensional bargain of agreement can be struck on the level of language.

What does this one mean by the statement *God exists,* and what does that one mean by the statement *God does not exist?* For sake of illustration, let us grossly simplify the complexities of human experience for a moment. Let us say that this person was brought up in a home environment in which parents were kind, loving, and trustworthy. For this one, a word symbol pointing to divine parenthood adequately expresses what is kind, loving, and trustworthy. Therefore, this person can feel comfortable with experiencing divine parenthood (God) as a picture of a spiritual experience of the world as trustworthy. Such a picture says, in effect, that this world is a world in which the path of acceptance, in which an ethic of trust and love, can be taken with confidence. For God exists!

Another person, in contrast, has had a negative experience of parenthood, including, perhaps, extremes of emotional, physical, or sexual abuse. For that one, a word symbol pointing to divine parenthood signifies that which is fearful, mistrustful, stifling of creativity. Therefore, that one finds it hard experience divine parenthood as symbol of the world as trustworthy and infused with love. Our earliest experiences of the world shape and contour (though do not determine) our most basic sense of life and environment. In the case of that person, basic reality has been experienced as cold, demanding, unforgiving, unloving. For that one, struggling toward the conclusion that God does not exist is a personally valid way of expressing a spiritual experience in which the world is no longer perceived as a place in which fear and mistrust create and rule; therefore one can live according to the path of acceptance, according to an ethic of love and trust, with full confidence. One may act with confidence and trust in this world because that great tyrant of tyrants in the sky is not real and does not exist![7]

The suggestion that agnostics and atheists be accepted with integrity in the gathered community of faith may deserve special attention. Many who are open to the idea that a genuine encounter with God might be found in many of the world's religious traditions continue to understand the spiritual struggle of this world as between believers and "unbelievers." My suggestion that agnostics and atheists whose lives demonstrate dedication to a pacifistic and ethically engaged way of being in the world can also be approached as people of faith draws from particular neo-orthodox perspectives. It can be placed theologically somewhere between the views of Karl Barth and Dietrich Bonhoeffer.

Barth understood human nature to be inherently religious and often supposed an opposition between religion and faith, in which faith is seen as given freely by God alone, while religion is seen variously as human attempts to mediate a connection to God apart from faith. Building on Barth, Bonhoeffer began to explore in his later writings the concept of a "religionless" Christianity. Although Bonhoeffer's martyrdom at the hands of the Nazi SS curtailed the full development of this idea, thus there is considerable disagreement among specialists as to just what he intended by the concept of a religionless Christianity, it is minimally clear that Bonhoeffer was exploring the idea that human nature may not be inherently religious, and that we might be coming into a time in which large numbers of human beings would live full and satisfying lives completely apart from religion as traditionally experienced. In this context, Bonhoeffer asked, what would faith mean?

Those who a few decades ago expected the gradual disappearance of religion have been surprised to see instead the continued and renewed vitality of religious yearnings and commitments, both traditional and nontraditional, among those very well-educated, scientifically and philosophically sophisticated, and materially successful groups of people whom it was thought would be the emerging religionless vanguard. The recent evidence, therefore, leans in favor of Barth's view that human nature is inherently religious. The type of religionless society Bonhoeffer and many others have explored in imagination has not materialized and, if anything, the world appears to be moving at a good clip in the opposite direction.

But Bonhoeffer also moved away from Barth in another area, in that Bonhoeffer, while agreeing that faith is given freely by God alone, also insists that faith can never be separated conceptually or existentially from obedience, understood as living one's life in a self-giving "life for others." Both Barth and Bonhoeffer recognized that faith, which comes only as a free gift from God, cannot be contained fully by any religion, including the Christian religion. However, Bonhoeffer was more clearly insistent than Barth on the proposition that if this is true, then we cannot locate faith in the religion or set of beliefs a person does or does not hold. Rather, faith is located in the lives of all those whose lives are animated by obedience, by discipleship, by living for others.

It is in this stream of reflection that we begin to make sense of the suggestion that the lives of many agnostics and atheists demonstrate their place among the people of faith. The spiritual struggle in this world is not between religions, or between "believers" and "unbelievers," but rather between faith/discipleship and nihilism. It is wrong, contrary to all evidence, to equate atheism with nihilism (as has become fashionable in much of current religiopolitical discourse.) Nihilism is located in actions that flow from a spirit of self-centered, all-others-be-damned behavior (an essential rejection of living one's life for others.)

We have certainly seen no lack of such behavior in our political, corporate, and religious leadership of late. And the pietistic/religious veneer it is too often given by the public relations "spin" once the public spotlight is placed on it only highlights its truly idolatrous character. But that spiritual struggle between faith and nihilism takes place not only in the corporate social sphere but also on a daily basis within each one of us. There we are confronted continually with God's call to faith, obedience, living for others, and the nihilistic pull to grab all we can for ourselves and hope no one notices.

This corporate, social, political, and personal struggle between faith and nihilism is not easily won for faith. Whether human nature is inherently religious or not, we know much in our nature that urges us toward grab-all-you-can nihilism. It can only be countered as people of faith come together and create an environment in which the life of obedience, discipleship, and living for others is discerned, nurtured, and encouraged.

Furthermore, this spiritual struggle continues without respect to race, creed, color, gender, sexual orientation, class, or religion. If for such reasons we exclude anyone evidently striving to heed that call to discipleship from the gathered people of faith, we not only cut them off from the discernment, encouragement, and nurturance of others who share their vision for humanity but also cut ourselves off from the comparable gifts they can offer us. In so doing, we support and placate the forces of nihilism in this world and in our own human nature.

A unity of people of faith based on a common moral and ethical stance in the world would fundamentally alter the structure of most churches. It would force the churches to state clearly the kind of moral and ethical stance in the world they expect of people of faith, removing the mask of religious ideology that now obscures the churches' social and moral expectations.[8] Such a unity would also make authoritarian structures within the churches much more difficult to maintain and rationalize.

Many people raised within various religious traditions have had the language and symbols of the religion passed on to them in ways that do not communicate an alignment of God with a cold and stifling status quo. It is easy and natural for these people to employ such language and symbols to express a spiritual experience of the world as trustworthy and infused with love. But for many others, the language and symbols of religious tradition have been inverted and express something opposite. The sacrificial death of Christ, for example, might be a powerful symbol of pacific trust in the power of love. But it is also a symbol under which whole populations have been slaughtered as well as inquisitions and witch hunts been carried out. It has been employed to sanctify brutal child abuse. It has been employed to sanctify even the cruelest systems of human slavery and bondage and as a symbol under which countless people have been frightened and bullied into social conformity.

It not surprising that large numbers of people in formerly Christian societies are now seeking to express spiritual experience through language and symbols other than those of the Christian tradition. This may take the form of borrowing language and symbols from other religions, or a stand of principled atheism toward the language and symbols of the Christian religion. Seeing this as an inevitable event in the demise of the Constantinian captivity of the Christian religion may allow people of faith to sympathize with, encourage, and interact creatively with such developments, keeping the doors of the church open to all people in our society drawn to the loving moral and ethical stance in the world they see there among people of faith.

In the absence of enforced conformity to creeds and doctrines, would total anarchy exist among people of faith in relation to expressions of spiritual experience? Is it possible to foster and encourage pluralism in the verbal expression of spiritual experience and still take language seriously? Is it finally the case that any and all use of language and symbols is of equal value?

Let us return to the illustration I began above. Both people give living evidence of a spiritual life in which trust and love are primary creative and sustaining principles. This one expresses living spiritual experience by saying God exists. That one expresses living spiritual experience by saying God does not exist. Within a gathering of people of faith, they contemplate their spiritual experience of the world. In freedom, without fear of censorship, they speak to the group of spiritual truth as they see it. It is understood by the group that such attempts to put spiritual experience into words are always experimental and tentative. Responses from the group are likewise experimental and tentative.

As spiritual truth is shared in this way, people of faith open up windows of deep communication with one another. People begin to understand more completely the biographical context within which each person works to formulate verbal symbolic expressions of living spiritual experience. As this learning process proceeds, the people in our illustration, who oppose each other so diametrically on the question of the existence of God, begin to understand better what each one means by the word symbol *God*. Eventually, they may be able to say to each other, "Aha! So that is what God means to you. Understanding that, and I can now more easily see why you would insist that God does (or does not) exist."

Both may continue to prefer their own way of saying it. But now both will have reached a higher level of understanding that neither could have reached alone without attempting seriously to understand the position of the other, or if they had simply divided themselves from one another as believer and unbeliever. Reaching of this higher level of communication and mutual understanding is one core value at the heart of communal gathering for a people of faith in a religiously pluralistic, post-Christian society.

There are a number of meeting structures that can help this kind of openness. In my personal experience, one of the best of these has been the silent meeting practiced among Quakers. Meeting for silence could be incorporated into the worship styles of many traditions, as well as other structural forms that help and encourage such openness among the people of faith, including those centered on sacramental liturgical worship and those intent on incorporating sensual and artistic expressions of faith. So long as meetings of the gathered people of faith are free from dogmatic expectations of uniformity, allowing freedom of expression and encouraging experimental approaches to language, contemplative spiritual life can be nurtured. As an increasing number of people seek to express their living spiritual experience of the world as trustworthy and infused with love in language and symbols other than those of the historic Christian tradition, new models for worship become valuable instruments in mission work and in ecumenical and interfaith discussion.

* * *

Doctrinal, confessional, and creedal pluralism, coupled with seeking of morally and ethically based unity for the gathered people of faith, has been presented here as a response to the new intellectual and sociopolitical situation, in which God is understood as fully incarnate in human history. It would be wrong, however, to assume that this approach to unity is itself new and has no historical precedent in Christian history.

The first generation for Christians certainly leaned toward a morally and ethically based unity. This was not only because of the strong influence of the Jewish religion upon the earliest Christians, although that was certainly part of it. Dogmatic formulations simply did not yet exist among them, nor was there an executive structure to enforce doctrinal orthodoxy. Their gatherings were open to all who chose to come, and biblical and contemporary literature makes it abundantly clear that doctrinal pluralism was the rule among the early Christians.[9]

Christianity was soon introduced into the Hellenistic environment, in which the political and mystical religions were in a decadent state. There were, to be sure, creative attempts on the part of Jews in diaspora to interpret Jewish monotheism within the context of the best Hellenistic religious and philosophical categories. And this created interest among non-Jews. But conversion to Judaism was a hard and complicated matter, demanding, among other things, circumcision of the male. Probably a large part of the reason Christianity became the major religion of the Roman world was that the Christian religion could more easily assimilate opposing mythologies in a plurality of doctrines.

Peter Munz's view of the relationship between experience, myth, and religion may help us understand what might have been involved.[10] Munz argued that there are two main axes in the symbol picture (mythology). One is that of a *male/creationist* myth of origins. The other is that of a *female/emanantal* myth of origins. By placing the redeemer myth within the symbol picture of creation, we arrive at a metaphysic of Absolute Love, or what Munz characterized as a metaphysic of Relationship. By placing the redeemer myth within the symbol picture of emanation, we arrive at a metaphysic of Absolute Consciousness, or what Munz characterized as a metaphysic of Solitude.

These are quite different conclusions, yet both can form the basis of a pacifistic moral and ethical stand in the world. A metaphysic of Relationship, or Absolute Love, leads in the direction of an action-oriented, messianically hopeful moral and ethical stand, in which forgiveness of evil overcomes the need for revenge or punishment because the future, rather than the past, is the all-embracing category. A metaphysics of Solitude, or Absolute Consciousness, leads in the direction of a contemplative ethical stand, in which pain and suffering are assimilated and negated in the higher consciousness that *All is One* and therefore without need for assigning blame, for revenge or compensation, for the present is the all-embracing category.

In both of these moral stands toward the world, we finally arrive at an ethic broadly characterized as pacifistic. Munz, furthermore, insisted that the two approaches are best understood as complementary, keeping issues of justice in front of the practitioner of Solitude and humbling the messianic pretensions of the practitioner of Relationship. The ideal is to keep these two basic approaches in creative tension with one another.

This is very similar to the creative tension implied by the view of God's kingdom as *present-future* oriented. In God's kingdom the absolute future becomes also the absolute present for those who will grasp it. But it is exactly the tendency to split the two apart that emerges when we attempt to find unity in language, in a common creed, set of doctrines, or an authoritarian interpretation of sacred texts. Unity based on a recognized common moral and ethical stand toward the world is more adequate to help keep these two perspectives in creative tension. It is difficult to accept the idea that no one symbol picture is more or less true than another, and that each can be positively assimilated. Yet there is evidence enough to question this bias that would force us to choose one or the other.

The witness of the early Christians. Early Christian theology placed the story of Jesus' death and resurrection within both creationist and emanantal frames of reference. Yet this pluralism also made it possible that Christianity would become the privileged religion of the disintegrating Roman Empire. The result of this was the tragic Constantinian inversion of Christian ideology from which we are only now slowly emerging.

On the other hand, had there been strict adherence to the male/creationist mythology among those who formed a sect within Palestinian Judaism, it is doubtful that this sect would have become more than a small and brief phenomenon, one among many other competing contemporary messianic sects. Furthermore, as Elaine Pagels demonstrated in her work on gnosticism,[11] later attempts to control the symbol picture within which Christ could be authoritatively preached were an essential element in the rise of an exclusively male-dominated hierarchy within the church.

Whether one greets it with joy or regret, the delegitimization of this hierarchical system of authority within the church is at the root of the present delegitimization of the Constantinian captivity of the Christian religion in general, a delegitimization which has been unfolding since the Enlightenment. This may be taken as a clear warning that attempts to control the symbol picture through which spiritual experience may legitimately be expressed can produce unintended secondary effects in the life of the church more destabilizing than constructive pluralism could ever be.

The witness of dissenting radicals such as Anabaptists and Quakers. Dissenting radicals such as Anabaptists and Quakers were mostly rooted firmly in biblical, evangelical theology—that is, the male/creationist frame of reference. Yet there are examples aplenty (one thinks here of such examples as Hans Denck and James Naylor[12]) in which there are appeals to the authority of the Spirit in each believer, to the Inner Light, that can hardly be constrained within that male/creationist frame of reference.

Recent scholarly attention focusing on the element of mysticism in the formative period of various dissenting groups has highlighted the fact that both poles in the symbol picture, a metaphysic of Relationship and a metaphysic of Solitude, were being cultivated simultaneously among them. It might even be argued that when one or the other approach crowded the other out, the dissenting group lost its socially critical edge—the price it paid for social respectability and political toleration.

The witness of pacifistic mystics. Pacifist mystics are present among all of the world's great religious traditions. This firm rooting in a metaphysic of Solitude is hard for those who do not have a mystical bent to understand. The religious experience of such mystics can be far removed from that of many people. However, it has been demonstrated in numerous contexts that the example and writings of these mystics, such as Meister Eckhart, have had a profound influence on reformers and radicals who are themselves more action-oriented. There is a preservative effect in the mystical experience of God which gives strength to those whose religious experience can more easily be expressed in terms of the metaphysics of relationship.

The witness of feminism. Feminist sisters have well articulated the pain and alienation they feel when expected to express their own spiritual experience exclusively in terms of the dominant male/creationist imagery. Dissenting groups have been far ahead of the Christian churches as a whole in terms of giving women more equal status—although this is done most often rather unconsciously, by lowering the authoritative status of all offices within the group.

In any case, the experience of the dissenting groups can be taken as a positive model. Many feminist theologians have been exploring female/emanantal imagery and have placed their fingers on the fact that while male/creationist imagery should lead to an ethics characterized by pacific love, it can and most often has been inverted and led to an ethic of power and domination. Males and females are learning to work together in mutual dialogue toward common imagery in their religious thinking. This does not mean sameness, but rather mutual respect.

A unity based on shared moral and ethical concern is more adequate for the gathered community within a pluralistic, post-Christian society than is an enforced creedal or doctrinal unity. There are various nonauthoritarian forms and structures within which this unity of practice could be cultivated. The pitfall of this approach is that it unquestionably elevates pluralism to a level at which we have not had much experience or an established track record. This can be frightening.

On the other hand, syncretistic exploration of symbols from various religious and secular traditions is already occurring in any case. The inversion of Christian language and symbols that—due to the Constantinian captivity of the Christian religion—often fills their ordinary meaning with Constantinian instead of Christian ideology makes this exploration necessary. It is a positive indication that people are seeking to find ways in which they can, with integrity, express their experience of the world as trustworthy and loving. The challenge, therefore, is not to hinder this exploratory process, but rather to create and to enhance structures within which the freedom spiritual exploration does not degenerate into isolated individualism. The emphasis on unity based on shared moral and ethical commitment is one way to keep people in dialogue as they attempt to give expression to their living spiritual experience of the world as trustworthy and loving.

Excursive Update—It is by now clear that for me, a crucial aspect of religious reflection centers on trying to understand the nature of religious beliefs and expressions. This is primarily an intellectual quest and is reflected in the style of gathered worship I have used to illustrate my views—primarily a picture of people sitting together and talking with each other. I want to stress strongly here that I fully endorse and support approaches to gathered worship in which talk may play an extremely limited role, and I also see such approaches as equally open to the perspective I have offered here.

In recent years, I have become very active in a worship activity known as the "Dances of Universal Peace." Gatherings of the Dances of Universal Peace consist of graceful, collective body movement while singing or chanting sacred phrases from many of the world's great religious traditions. The theological emphasis in these phrases is the unitary aspect of God found in all people. I think of this activity as "communal body prayer," linked in my view to other examples of contemplative exercises, from pilgrimage to walking the Labyrinth Circles, that many Christians are now exploring and finding meaningful and useful in constructing a renewed sense of spiritual depth and awareness amid our harried lives.

I mention the Dances of Universal Peace here not because I recommend it unreservedly to everyone. I recognize as valid, rather, the criticism that what I offer here is, for the most part, a highly intellectualized vision of human spirituality. The Dances of Universal Peace are one example of a style of gathered worship quit opposite to this highly intellectualized approach, and I want to indicate clearly that I see it as compatible with the perspectives I advocate throughout these pages. Although I can best articulate the intellectualized approaches, there are others who can best articulate other ways of proceeding. That is why I want to emphasize that I see these views as mutually supportive and supplementary, not as mutually contending or contradictory, approaches.

7

IN VIEW OF OTHER RELIGIONS

We live in a world in which we rub shoulders daily with people of other faith traditions. Further, these are people we have learned to know personally, to respect and appreciate, people who we see exhibit a high sense of personal and social values—honesty, integrity, progressive social commitment, family principles—that we have come to associate with being the fruits of a sincere spiritual connection. In this chapter I want sketch out an application of the most basic insights that have emerged from my reflections to relationships with people of other faith traditions. In doing so, I think two preliminary comments will be helpful.

First of all, most of what I have to say in this chapter was originally formed within the of a context of being a young student from a sectarian and—at least in theory—significantly dissenting Christian faith tradition. I was not then having my thinking shaped within a setting of reflection on relationships with people of other-than-Christian faith traditions but a student trying to navigate a completely unfamiliar ecumenical environment. Raised in a small, predominantly Mennonite town in Indiana, I had attended a Mennonite high school, two Mennonite colleges, and a Mennonite seminary by the time I was twenty-four before I lived for any significant amount of time outside of a predominantly Mennonite context. Since then, however, for the past quarter-century, I have lived in Budapest, Vienna, New York, Philadelphia, largely outside of Mennonite enclaves. I would easily go weeks and months without a face-to-face encounter with another Mennonite. Even then, the encounter would be by conscious choice only.

This lapse into personal biography demonstrates that for me, a major issue in my adult life was originally not so much how to get along with those of other-than-Christian faith traditions, though it did include this. Rather, the issue originally was how to relate ecumenically to people of other Christian traditions significantly different than my own. Only later did I recognize that the ecumenical social vision I had hammered out, a vision of one humanity made up of people of many different faiths, had rather direct application to situations of inter-religious pluralism as well. In short, my understanding of relationships in an interfaith context grows from and is a direct extension of my understanding of inter-Christian, ecumenical relationships.

The second point is that I am consciously presenting my reflections in this area as simply one view to be considered. I am not insisting on my view as the only valid one. Statements I make in the following chapter should necessarily be taken as devastating criticism of any particular church program.

For example, in Christian mission, I favor programs aimed at ministering to the economic, social, emotional, psychological, and spiritual needs of others as these are understood in the context of sharing a vision of people living together in peace and mutual respect. I do not favor programs that move among other-than-Christian people with the specific aim and intention of seeking conversions to the Christian religion and measure their effectiveness by the numbers of such converts. This does not mean, however, that I want all such programs shut down or am judging the value of people who devote their lives to such programs. My comments are intended, rather, to indicate what I support, with the time and resources of which I have been made steward, in full knowledge and awareness that other people are drawn to support other projects.

Contemporary religious reflection is in large part contoured by the experience of positive interaction with people of other religious traditions. A dialogically open mind was always a virtue, but as we enter the third millennium, it is more than a virtue. Just a generation ago, it was possible for most Christian people in America and Europe to ignore other religions. Other religions were confronted only in slide presentations of missionaries returning from the foreign fields of service. By our time, however, North America and Europe themselves have become foreign mission fields, and city streets and airports at times are jammed with adherents of numerous religions, each seeking converts. Once it might have seemed odd to hear a discussion in which an Asian Baptist and an African Roman Catholic relived in vigorous discussion the divisions that took place in sixteenth-century Europe. Now it is common to find in university settings, at least, heated debate in which American or European converts to Buddhism relive in vigorous debate divisions that took place in Asia a millennium ago.

In the absence of an officially sanctioned religion, America especially has been a place in which hundreds, even thousands, of religions, sects, heresies, divisions, and groups can flourish. Europe is increasingly experiencing the same phenomenon. On both continents, immigration from Near and Far Eastern lands have greatly increased the numbers of inhabitants who adhere to Islam, Hinduism, and Buddhism, adding to the number converted to forms of these religions from the native population.

The speed of travel and communications has made us a truly global community. Each and every culture is affected and influenced by other cultures. The resulting cultural pluralism present in all areas of life is especially evident in the religious sphere. The average person now probably knows more about other religions than most religious scholars did in previous generations. The holy books of other-than-Christian religions are easily available in inexpensive trade paperback editions, and indications are that these sell well. The full tide of religious pluralism is upon us and cross-fertilization of ideas and practices is occurring apace. My hope is that we will encounter this not as a threat to overcome but as opportunity to be grasped.

* * *

Conservative Christian theology persists in teaching that Christianity is universally the one true religion.[1] Evaluations of other religions range from the charitable view that these are sincere errors to the harder line that they are demonic deceptions. Especially in America, conservative theology has been known for its battle over the Bible, its fortress-like and sometimes auto-cannibalistic defense of biblical authority. The Bible is viewed as the one true revelation of God for all people. The Bible must be seen as infallible, as free from any errors of commission and omission. Therefore, whatever view of other religions we hold, the conservatives insist that view must come directly from the Bible.

It is true that a direct reading of the Bible does not yield much ground for dialogical openness toward other religions. Narratives in the Hebrew Bible tell mainly of heroic individual, family, and national struggles to repel the syncretistic temptations from the religions of neighbors and conquerors. Critical scholarship informs us that the religious beliefs and practices of the ancient Hebrews were in fact molded by such syncretistic interaction, but this is rarely acknowledged explicitly in the actual biblical text.

In the Christian testament as well, we find narratives of the struggles of the early church in the Palestinian and Greco-Roman contexts. The clearly intended purpose of these narratives is proclamation and proselytism. Judaism, from which the Christian religion came, is progressively caricatured as a negative foil to Christian truth in these writings. Paul's appearance at Mars Hill in Athens might be taken as a lesson in dialogue, but again, his clear purpose was proclamation and proselytism rather than mutual exchange and mutual learning.

Whatever sanction one finds in the Bible for sympathetic treatment of other religions and dialogical openness toward other religions comes only through reflective inference on the moral and ethical ideals found there, rarely from the text itself. For those disinclined toward sympathetic toleration in the first place, these reflective inferences are simply submerged in direct readings of holy wars, prophetic condemnations of syncretism, Christian invectives against "the Jews," and visions of a final Armageddon in which the foes of God are exterminated once and for all. Reading the Bible as the one true revelation of the one true God has not equipped conservative theology with a sympathetic doctrine of other religions.

If the Bible is viewed as the one true revelation of God, what can conservatives say of the holy books of other religions? Again responses vary. More charitably, this approach must see these holy books as human inventions on the same level as other books of human authorship. They may contain good stories, even useful advice, just as many books contain useful advice. But it must always be maintained that the Bible is qualitatively different. Less charitable views of holy books of other religions are also written by conservative theologians. In their view, there is rather direct movement from the finality of God's revelation in the Bible, to the absolute uniqueness of Christ, to the conclusion that other religions are false and cannot lead to salvation. The only aim of the gospel can be conversion, the hope that people of other faiths will give up their false religions and become Christian converts. Where dialogue and learning from other faiths is encouraged in conservative circles, such as in the statement of the International Congress on World Evangelism, its purpose is clearly as a tool or tactic useful in leading adherents of other religions to Christian conversion.[2] Conversion-minded Christians must understand the needs of people so as to more effectively convert them to Christianity. Sensitive listening is a tool or tactic for proselytism.

Although certainly more academically sophisticated, the neo-orthodox approach toward other religions characterized by Karl Barth[3] also edged toward many positions and statements similar to that of conservatives. In reacting against the humanism of nineteenth century liberal theology, Barth set out to describe a radicalized Christology. To know nothing but Christ and Christ crucified was Barth's answer to confusion of his time. Barth insisted that we know nothing of God except as God reveals Godself in Jesus Christ. The source for our knowledge of Jesus Christ is the Bible, particularly the Christian New Testament.

Once these elements are in place, it mattered little that Barth and his followers tried studiously to avoid propositional statements concerning the exact nature of God's revelation in the Bible, nor that they refused the conservative pet phrases concerning that revelation. The stage was clearly set in any case for an essentially negative reading of other religious faiths. Barthians stressed the absolute center of God's revelation of Godself in Jesus Christ as mediated through the New Testament. Once one is painted into that corner, there is little room for movement in the encounter with other faiths. God can only be known by self-revelation. God is revealed only in Jesus Christ. What then of other faiths?

Barth said that *religion* was humankind's attempt to find God. But this effort is doomed to failure since God can only be known by self-revelation. Therefore, the religions cannot lead to salvation, nor are they a way to find God. At best they are useless. At worst they actually hinder one from recognizing God's self-revelation and are therefore a form of rebellion and unbelief against God.

There are nuances of difference between the Barthians and the conservatives, however. For although Barth's radical Christology does not prepare us for a sympathetic and dialogically open approach to other religions, it did allow Barth to hear a word of prophetic criticism concerning Christian culture that conservatives mostly miss. Barth was much more concerned to deny that knowledge of God could come through rational scientific method and historical critical investigation than to deny that knowledge of God could come through faithful belief and practice of other of the world's great religions.

It should be noted that Barth did not work out his earlier view of other religions in a context of close acquaintance with other religions. There is even some evidence that later in his life, when he did begin to consider the place of other religions in theological context, Barth began to backpedal from earlier negative pronouncements. Barth's earlier view was mainly an implied byproduct of his scathing theological criticism of cultural Christianity (i.e., the remnant echoes of the Constantinian captivity of the Christian faith still quite evident in the Europe of Barth's era.) Barth insisted that whatever negative judgments were given about the world's religions, these same judgments applied equally, perhaps even primarily, to the Christian church itself.

If one takes that pronouncement seriously, Barth cannot be accused of simple cultural chauvinism. Barth's radical Christology was primarily a criticism of the Christian church. Barth's theology has been influential among culturally and politically critical religious thinkers, including Mennonite theologians and activists who were direct or indirect students of Barth. However, his is a theology hardly suited to the present situation, as we attempt to make our way peacefully among the labyrinth of religious pluralism.

* * *

Moderate ecumenical theologians have been unhappy with the arrogant tone of condemnation toward other religions most often found among the conservatives and the Barthians. Ecumenical theology, following the tone set by the World Council of Churches and by the Second Vatican Council, has been exploring positions in which other religious traditions can be viewed in a positive light, allowing for mutual respect between the traditions. While a major stride forward, moderate ecumenical theology is undermined by its reluctance to criticize the traditional demands of particularity found in Christian theology and Christology.

Moderate ecumenical theology usually begins by outlining a rather strong, perhaps exaggerated, distinction between *natural* revelation—knowledge of God open to every human being—and *special* revelation, knowledge of God that God must impart. The more of God known through channels of natural revelation, the more knowledge of God we can legitimately ascribe to other religions. The main thing other religions lack, according to this view, is the special revelation of God found only in Christianity. What can be known through natural revelation, from the creation itself, is that God exists, that God is good, and that the creation, including human beings, is in need of redemption. Therefore, other religions can be seen as pathways toward Christian redemption, as preparation for the specific Christian revelation concerning the means God has chosen for redemption of the world.

This means there is potentially much in other religions to affirm. Christians may even learn from other religions in areas of general revelation, the knowledge of God open to all people. On this level, there can be true mutual appreciation. But this view must finally insist that on the level of specific revelation, on the level of God's plan of salvation for the world, religions other than Christianity will ultimately fall short. Other religious traditions are in need of *fulfillment* by Christian revelation. Other religious paths may lead to the gates of salvation, but only Christian revelation allows entry into those gates.

Although moderate ecumenical theologians are less enthusiastic about drawing conclusions about the damnation of people of other faiths than their conservative colleagues, their theology does imply that those outside the Christian religion are excluded from salvation, however that is defined. Where salvation is clearly pictured as having to do with eternal life after death, the problem centers on how it would be possible for God to damn eternally the majority of humanity who, because of accident of birth, never had the chance to hear the Christian message. Where salvation is viewed in more historical categories, it still makes God's will seem unjustly arbitrary to insist that only Christianity is the route to salvation. Furthermore, such exclusivist tendencies contradict what has been learned about the complex social organization of non-Christian societies, many of which exhibit at least as keen a sense of social justice as Christian societies.

Faced with such contradictions, some moderate theologians have sought ways out of the impasse their adherence to Christian particularity created. They have sought to discern how Christians might affirm that true salvation can be found also in other religious traditions.

Probably the best known such attempt has been that of Karl Rahner's idea of the *anonymous* Christian.[4] Rahner began by asserting God's will that all people should find salvation. Through the creation itself God reveals Godself, therefore all people have received revelation. All revelation leads to salvation. Therefore all religions can be seen as part of God's plan of salvation for humanity. People who follow a religious tradition other than Christianity, but who lead exemplary moral lives and truly worship God from within their own religious tradition, may be viewed as Christians, even if they themselves neither know of Christianity nor accept the label personally. We may view them as anonymous Christians.

Rahner's views follow from an expanded Christology in which Christ is no longer seen as confined to the Christian tradition. Similarly, Hans Kung[5] has asked us to abandon *ecclesiocentrism* in the name of this expanded Christology, a Christology affected by Karl Barth as well as Roman Catholic sources. Jesus Christ can be seen as the *norm for all people* without assuming one finds him only among Christians. Other religions are the ordinary way of salvation for humanity, while Christianity represents the extraordinary way for the people of the Christian faith.

But what Rahner and Kung give to other religions on the one hand, they seem to take back on the other hand. For both there is a time-limitation on the way of salvation through other religions. In one way or another, at one time or another, other religions will cease to be ways of salvation and be displaced by Christianity, or at least by explicit recognition that the Christian God is God of everyone. Rahner seems to say that the time comes when a person first hears the Christian gospel. Kung, more attentive to the social channels through which a religious message travels, says it will happen only when Christianity has become enough of the part of a culture for a person to be presented with an authentic choice between the Christian message and that of the other religion. In either case, however, the time is limited. The ideology of Christian particularism finally displaces the reality of pluralism in moderate ecumenical theology.

A theologian who has moved beyond the moderate ecumenical position is John Hick.[6] John Hick uses an analogy from astronomy and speaks of a "Copernican Revolution" in theology, which comes about in response to modern pluralism. In Hick's analogy, moderate ecumenical theology remains confined to a sun-centered, Ptolemaic universe. While the challenge of new questions can be met in this theology by adding cosmic circles, which enlarge the scope of the system, the system itself remains bound to a center. Christological particularism, the myth of God uniquely incarnate in Jesus Christ, is this center. So long as theology clings to this central doctrine, it can never truly accept and move comfortably within the pluralistic matrix of thought.

In contrast, John Hick proposes a theocentric rather than christocentric theology. The true object of all religious devotion, God as Godself, or, in Hick's preferred terms, the "Eternal One," is not and cannot be known and articulated directly, but always and only through mediation of religions. No religion can give more than a partial picture of the Eternal One. Thus for example it would be possible to affirm that Jesus Christ is an absolutely true revelation of God without having to insist on the opposite, that all other revelations of God in other religions are necessarily false or even inferior. Knowledge of God in other religions may broaden the Christian understanding of God without competing with it or attempting to displace it.

In his historical reconstruction, Hick makes much of Karl Jaspers' "axial period," roughly 800 to 200 BCE. It was during this era that, in China, India, the Middle East, and the Mediterranean worlds, the major religious traditions of humankind crystallized out of their tribalistic and animistic origins. During this period the Eternal One pressed in on humanity, and new spiritual insights were gained in cultures unconnected with one another in any direct sense. The spiritual insights which took strong root in one culture may differ from those that took strong root in another.

Therefore, one religious tradition may emphasize the personal nature of God and hold the impersonal qualities of God as an undercurrent. Another culture may emphasize the impersonal nature of God and hold the personal qualities as an undercurrent. Such surface contradictions are important but not final. For Hick feels that especially in the practical area of worship, it is possible to see that people are responding, within a tradition which mediates language, methods, and so forth, to the same Eternal One. God has many names.

From Hick's perspective, one may wholly affirm the truth and integrity of all religious traditions. One may enter into true dialogue with those of other faiths without any hidden agenda of proselytism or conversion. One may view the teachings of other religious traditions as opportunities to expand the horizons of one's own understanding. People of all religions can be seen as one family, united by the theocentrism of each tradition.

* * *

Hick's theocentric view commendably creates a vision beyond an implied hierarchy of religions, reflecting a nuanced and sensitive understanding of other religions. My own reflections can best be articulated as an expansion on the basic insights of Hick's theocentrism. Hick begins with the wide variety of human religious experience and practice and, looking at this data cumulatively, produces an expanded conception of God that best accounts for the data. While my reflections are compatible with Hick's view, my concern, reflecting an anthropological bias, has always been less to construct new models of God *per se* and more to notice what this variety of data tells us about human beings.

Specialists in the phenomenological study of religion have noticed significantly recurring patterns in the ways in which human beings suffer and interpret religious experience. These recurring patterns can be arranged schematically to elucidate the archetypal nature of the basic categories of religiosity. Though it is not the only such effort, for classroom use, introducing respect for spiritual diversity to social work professionals, I have found the schematic analysis of Streng, Lloyd, and Allen[7] to be very valuable. This analysis contains eight broad but quite distinct ways of being religious. (Cf. appendix 1)

1. Personal Experience of the Holy
2. Creation of Community Through Myth and Ritual
3. Daily Living That Expresses the Cosmic Law
4. Spiritual Freedom Through Discipline (mysticism)
5. Achieving an Integrated Self Through Creative Interaction
6. Social and Economic Justice as an Ultimate Concern
7. New Life Through Technocracy
8. Fullness of Living Through Sensuous Expression

Each of these broad categories are shown to contain a basic worldview, a mode of being in the world of experience, that includes a sense of—

The Problem (what is wrong in the world);

The Answer (what should be done to rectify the problem);

The Means of Individual Appropriation (how and in what ways the individual participates in the redemption process);

The Means as Expressed Socially (how and in what ways the group or community participates in the redemption process.)

More categories could be conceived to expand this schematic analysis. Exhaustiveness of analysis is not most important here. Important to notice is that this is not an analysis of any particular religion but of human religiosity itself, archetypal ways of being religious. These categories also easily incorporate many prominent *secular* paths for pursuing meaning and truth—for example, the pursuit of scientific discovery or political ideology.[8]

What I find especially useful in this schema for reflecting on religious phenomena is that we see quickly that the primary sticking points of religious understanding and dialogue may not necessarily be *between* the religions so much as *within* the religions. A Christian mystic, for example, may be able to find common grounds for communication much more easily with a Muslim Sufi or a Buddhist Zen practitioner than with a fellow Christian following a decidedly nonmystical path.

With this basic notion in mind, I want to make a few suggestions and observations. I am not claiming studied knowledge in what follows, but rather setting forth a few ideas for further consideration.

If we tentatively entertain the conception that religiosity is an aspect of being human, originating from within the human sphere, we may hypothesize that these analytical categories represent not only human ways of being religious, but more broadly basic ways of being human; that is, basic types of human personality.[9] It suggests that people of a given personality style will be drawn into (a cluster of) certain styles of religious expression, whereas people of quite different personality styles will drawn to (a cluster of) different styles of religious expression. However, the spectrum of ways of being religious will be present in some degree within all religions, just as any religion will encompass people of all styles of personality.

A given society tends to privilege (and therefore produce more of) certain personality styles. For example, in contemporary America, we tend to privilege (and therefore produce more of) personality styles with a high degree of such traits as competitiveness, individuation, achievement, acquisitiveness, material desire, sense of individual entitlement, aggression, and ambition.[10] A different society (for example, communal Hutterite or Navaho) will tend to privilege (and therefore produce more of) personality styles of quite different character traits. The privileged or dominant ways of being religious in a particular time and place tends to be those corresponding to the personality styles privileged within the society of that time and place.

Viewed historically, and recognizing that the major world religions were nurtured over centuries and even millennia within the societies of distinctive civilizations, we see that one given religion tends to become characterized by certain dominant clusters of ways of being religious, with other ways taking a subdominant role within that religion. What is dominant in one religion may be subdominant in another religion, and vice versa. Therefore, we might say in very broad and general terms (while fully acknowledging all the exceptional cases in point to the generalization) that the historically Far-Oriental-cultural religions tend toward predominantly *inward* looking clusters of ways of being religious that are subdominant in the historically Euro-cultural religions. Likewise, the historically Euro-cultural religions tend toward predominantly *outward* looking clusters of ways of being religious that are subdominant in historically Far-Oriental-cultural religions.

A similar dynamic occurs *within* the cultural, national, ethnic, and denominational subgroups within a given religion. Some characteristic ways of being religious will dominate while others are subdominant. The dominant religious style of a given subgroup may be distinctively different than the religious styles of other nearby subgroups, even within one religion. While both are Christian, one can easily see differences in dominant religious styles between, say, Lebanese Orthodox congregations and those of American Southern Baptists. This same analysis could be extended to differences within one stream of one religion. The literature is rife with discussions of the differences in style (especially related to acceptance of hierarchical authority) between American Roman Catholics and other Roman Catholics. Similarly, I heard a reputable Mennonite historian lecture on the noticeable differences between Dutch-German and Swiss-German Mennonites (differences that would be invisible to any but the most trained non-Mennonite eyes.)

When a person is raised within a subgroup privileging a distinctive religious style that does not meet the emotional, psychological, spiritual, or social needs of that person, the person may be attracted to an entirely different religion perceived as identified with a more compatible style of being religious. Or it may be that the person will be attracted to a different subgroup within his or her own religion that exhibits a more compatible religious style.[11] There is a creative experimentation with religious practices, rituals, music, liturgies, and even language for worship of other religions and religious subgroups taking place in our post-Christian society. Such experimentation reflects our growing awareness, coming from the experience of dialogical openness with those of other traditions and backgrounds, that valid ways of being religious are much broader than the dominant styles with which we were raised.

On the whole, we may expect that the outcome of this creative experimentation will be less that of conversion from one religion to another and more that of finding freedom to explore those subdominant, even neglected, ways of being religious that were subdominant or neglected within one's own faith.[12] In a religiously pluralistic society, it may make more sense to deemphasize thinking of mission work as encouraging religious conversions to one's own religion. It may be more productive to think of mission work as facilitating creative experimentation with the many ways of being religious as well as helping others explore avenues for expression of a religious style compatible with the subdominant channels of their own religion.

* * *

I agree with Hick that God has many names and is manifested in many equally valid ways across the spectrum of human religions. But I also agree with the conservatives that there are true and false images of God. As we saw in an earlier chapter, the view of God a person holds is crucial and can have direct public consequences. That image sets the parameters of action. It both establishes and reflects a particular value system. There are both true and false Gods; Gods of compassion, justice, and nonviolence, but also Gods of injustice, violence, and bigotry. We must seek to establish true Gods and maintain atheism in the face of false Gods. Which Gods are true and which are false, however, do not correspond simply with any particular religion. Spiritual discernment must be based on the moral and ethical consequences of belief in particular Gods within particular situations.

I do reject the nebulous conclusion that any and all religious expressions are equally good or equally bad, equally useful or equally useless. Criteria must apply in sorting through the multitude of religious responses of humankind. At their best, religious commitments and expression allow each human being to feel recognized and confirmed as significant and as having a sense of personal meaning; they nurture in each human being those virtues of spiritual substance manifested in attitudes of tolerance, respect, critical self-esteem, love for others, generosity, concern for justice, a sense of being a world citizen, and a sense of responsibility and desire to live peacefully with all species within the earth's ecosphere. Such criteria help the creation of social arrangements fostering a vital environment of purpose and values based on a firm sense of social connectedness.

These are three aspects of one continuous movement toward social maturity. In our situation of global crises, in which holocausts of war, of genocide, and of ecological collapse stare us menacingly in the face, it represents a movement toward species survival as well. Spiritual discernment begins as we keep this movement toward social maturity on our mental horizon. Religious expressions that foster movement in the direction of social maturity are to be encouraged. Those tending to move against this current of social maturity are to be questioned and discouraged.

To summarize, there is no one conception of God that is the universally and transcendentally correct view by which all others can be measured or ranked. Any conception of God that helps people in their movement along this continuum of social maturity is true. Any conception causing stagnation is false.

Second, since what we seek is movement along a continuum of social maturity, we must expect that individual conceptions of God will change over time, sometimes dramatically. We may take here as apt analogy those theories of moral development which speak of stages.[13] We would not expect, for example, a six-year-old to give the same answers as a teenager to moral questions of right and wrong. We expect them to be at different stages of moral development and sophistication. An eighteen-year-old who answers as a six-year-old would be seen as having stagnated. Likewise, were a six-year-old to answer as an eighteen-year-old, we would have reason to doubt if the child really understood what he or she was saying. Therefore, though the two would disagree as to the specifics of what is right or wrong in a given set of circumstances, we can affirm both of them in the truth of their moral reasoning and judgments without lapsing into moral relativism.

Similarly, we may affirm the truth in a conception of God, let us say, as "The one watching you all the time and who punishes you when you do wrong," offered by a child at the stage of moral development in which she or he is struggling to internalize basic rules of social behavior. Such a God is a meaningful aid in this process of internalizing behavioral impulse control. By acting as a sort of omniscient externalized and reified conscience, such a God is helpful to the child in moving along the continuum of social maturity. But such a view coming from an otherwise mentally developed adult might signal spiritual stagnation.

Third, and closely related to what has just been said, a view of God needed and necessary at one stage of a person's spiritual life for dramatic behavioral change cannot be universalized. Here I think of conversations I have had with people who have been substance abusers or hardened prisoners. The testimony of such people generally points toward conceptions of God quite different from the one I find meaningful. The conception of God central in my life might not have sufficient psychological, emotional, or spiritual intensity to turn such people from self-destructive social pathology. Is this not proof even on my own terms, I have asked myself, that their conceptions of God are somehow more true than my own?

Yet I have come to see that I can affirm the conceptions of God in the preaching of a skid row missionary or prison minister without assuming this view must be true for everyone at all times. Our only criteria can be whether a particular conception of God, in the time and place it appears, is helping people along the continuum of social maturity. Similarly, I have met many people who have had dramatic religious experiences, then some years later feel guilty because they have lost something of that experience. "God used to be so close to me! I talked to God in prayer all the time. Now I just don't feel that way anymore. What went wrong?"

Their conception of God surely has changed from the time of that intense religious experience. But that does not necessarily mean they have lost anything. The question to be examined, rather, is whether the conception of God they now hold is now helping them along this continuum of social maturity. More than once I have heard people speak of their belief in God and God's punishment as the only thing that keeps them from a life of drinking, drugs, sexual indulgence, and crime—and this twenty years after an initial Christian conversion, now that they have for two decades been clean and sober, with loving spouse and family, holding a place of responsibility in the community. Perhaps some in that situation are always only a hair's breadth, one crisis of religious doubt, from tossing it all over and returning to the carousing life. I doubt it, though I understand that this sort of formulation is expected and encouraged in some religious circles. I tend to think that if such people were more honest with themselves about their current motivations, they would see that they have moved far along the continuum of social maturity from those earlier days; they might even grow if faced with a crisis of religious doubt and resulting alterations in their conceptions of God.

Since what we seek is movement and growth in social maturity in our conceptions of God, we need not assume all humans must move and grow at the same speed. We need not even assume all humans will reach the same understanding of God. Even though we speak of movement and growth, we are not assuming an evolutionary pattern that envisions a hierarchal sophistication in conceptions of God. An astrophysicist may well have a very different view of the universe from mine. But my rudimentary understanding of the universe does not necessarily mean stagnation according to the criteria under discussion. If my goal were to become an astrophysicist, and I had learned nothing more about quarks and black holes in my years than I in fact have, then that would surely mean stagnation. But as it is not my goal to be an astrophysicist, I am not held to such standards in this area.

Likewise, specialists in philosophy or theology need not assume that everyone must come to view spiritual matters with the refined sophistication of the specialist. Just as the astrophysicist will have a different understanding of the universe from that commonly shared by most of us, so the religious specialist may have a different view of God than others in the congregation.[14] But this need not imply in either case an elitism or hierarchy of views. It is rather an embrace of pluralism.

Finally, in our view of other religions, we should not primarily seek conversion from one religion to another, although this may come as a secondary byproduct and need not necessarily be discouraged. We should avoid ranking religions according to some external value system. We need not even expect some unification of the religious traditions on some higher, transcendental level.[15]

What we should do, as an effort of Christian mission, is minister mutually to the economic, emotional, and spiritual needs of fellow human beings. We should share the vision we have glimpsed, through the embodiment of divine truth in the life and teaching of Jesus, of diverse people living together in peace and justice, while respectfully encouraging others in movement and growth along this continuum of social maturity. And we should seek sources for such movement and growth from *within* each of the religious traditions.

8

FINAL REFLECTIONS

*I*n this book, I used the terms *post-Christian* and *post-Constantinian* more or less interchangeably. This was by design. My sense is that many Christian people experience a negative reaction when they hear talk of a post-Christian society, as if this were an anti-Christian society in which Christians have no legitimacy. This is not what the term means, at least in my usage. It designates a society in which the power of the institutional Christian religion to act in mutual support of state power and policy has dissolved in favor of policy that seeks to reflect the diversity of spiritual and moral commitments within the population.

* * *

The movement toward a post-Christian culture began in the Western world at least by the sixteenth century, and the Enlightenment gave it considerable philosophical momentum. In European societies, the uncoupling of the Christian religion from state power resulted in widespread secularism and indifference toward active participation in the institutional forms of Christianity among the indigenous population. In North America, such a trend has been much less prominent, or at least much slower in developing. Nevertheless, the decline in an ability of American churches to define for all the common sense morality, and the marked reluctance of the state to enforce the churches' morality on all citizens, has created noticeable anxiety among many American Christians concerning the continuing movement into a post-Christian era.

When we understand this as the continuing movement toward a post-Constantinian era, much of that anxiety may be allayed. Especially for those of us who continue the free church/believers church tradition of Protestantism, it is at the heart of our vision that the system of a mutually supportive relationship between the Christian religion and the power politics of the state (symbolized by the first Christian Emperor, Constantine) was a tragic mistake in the first place. As we move into a post-Christian era, my hope is that we will be able to encounter this as a positive opportunity for spiritual growth, in which we learn finally what it means to be salt and yeast in the cultural mix but never expecting to be the whole loaf. The alternative (as we already see in some quarters of the churches) is to scheme nostalgically to hang onto at least symbolic vestiges of ebbing social and political power. This route is a waste of time and energy, and, from a free church/believers church perspective, profoundly unfaithful to the Christian message.

In the original edition of this book, I leaned toward the assumption that continued secularism was the most likely description of the future of religion in a post-Christian era. I drew heavily on what sociologists call the "secularization thesis."[1] Looking back now, I think I was too strongly influenced by the European experience. (I had at that time just returned from eight years in Europe.) Presently, I am less convinced that continued secularization is the most probable direction American society will move in a post-Christian era. If Ernest Becker and other observers are correct that the religious urge emerges directly from the human need to make sense of life, to maintain purpose and meaning in the face of life's limitations and death, then we must conclude we are as religious by nature as we are mortal by nature.

Although the data is subject to various interpretations, it is worth noting that recent research appears to indicate that the urge toward spiritual transcendence is imprinted in the neural pathways of the normal human brain itself.[2] The Psalmist (Ps. 42) intended no more than figure of speech in likening the animal need for water to the human need for relationship with God. It is quite a thought that recent neurological investigation may suggest this is more like an empirical, scientific description.

* * *

Even if it were universally accepted, however, that humans are religious by nature, that the secularization thesis is fully-wrongheaded, and that the totalitarian efforts of the past century to wipe out religion were not only enormously pathological crimes against humanity but also terribly bad science, this would still be mixed comfort. For as we have seen earlier, true and false gods both fulfill the human urge for spiritual transcendence. It may even be that in the short run idols are more attractive. For, to put the ideas of the ancient Psalmist into the words of a more recent psalmist, "everybody's got a hungry heart." There is a yearning, a deep sense of emptiness, guilt, and inadequacy in each one of us that cries out for fulfillment and completion.

Contemporary Buddhist philosopher David Loy[3] character-izes the yearning as a "lack of Being," an intuition that the "Self is unreal." Spiritual Director Ronald Rolheiser[4] speaks of it as a "Holy Longing," placing it at the center of Christian spirituality itself. St. John of the Cross[5] wrote of a *Dark Night of the Soul.* Kierkegaard[6] wrote of a *Sickness Unto Death.* Existential philoso-phers refer to it as an "inward sense of despair." Whatever it is called, it is deeply felt by any person willing to slow down long enough to let the defenses melt away.

This phenomenon intrigued Ernest Becker, who wanted to understand it scientifically and for whom it increasingly became the focus of his anthropological work. By now an enormous amount of literary, clinical, and empirical evidence is congealing in support of Becker's basic theory—that the concrete reality un-derlying this phenomenon is the ability of the human mind to re-flect back on itself as object and recognize its impending death, its own mortality. The human spiritual nature, which includes religion but also encompasses most of what we associate with the higher aspects of cultural life, arises from the psyche's need to mask itself from itself, to help the psyche in repressing and deny-ing the fact of its own mortality.

The mechanism behind the human sense of lack, guilt, and inadequacy was largely unknown and explored only in mytho-logical language. Its explication in empirical concepts and cate-gories makes it somewhat more possible that people will be able to take rational control and become less puppets of their uncon-scious desires.

However, this is by no means certain. The reasons for this re-late to why false gods seem to have the constant upper hand, why idols are so attractive. Because this sense of guilt, lack, and inadequacy arises in the first place from a real condition of powerlessness in the face of death, we will always have a strong tendency to confuse overwhelming social power, which in the final analysis is the power to execute violence, with divine power. That is, our *natural* conceptions of God, those we are drawn to unconsciously, will most likely contain heavy elements of divine violence. *God's will be done!* without too much concern about who gets hurt in the process.

Second, the idols may only offer illusions of mortality transcendence, but at least they offer that. The true gods, for the most part, offer only the possibility of acceptance of one's mortal condition.[7] The promise of more abundant living pales compared to actual wealth, fame, and power over actual others in the here and now. Even the vicarious experience of the common person through adulation or resentment (two sides of one coin) of the wealthy, the famous, and the powerful will seem concrete in comparison. Yes, the transcendence of the false gods is ultimately false and empty, enslaving rather than freeing, but it may take years for the tarnish to appear on the glimmering idols. For the most part, however, this wisdom of experience is not cumulative and must be learned all over again in each generation.

For these reasons, the invitation of true gods that we live together in peace, guided by communal anticipations of justice and equality, will always appear rather weak. Such an invitation is never backed by an implied threat of top-down enforcement.

Setting the human problem up this sharply—that we will never overcome our violence unless and until we overcome our urge for immortality—seems to create an impasse. How can we ever overcome the urge for immortality? This may be selling ourselves short, however. I have personally seen in my work with hospice patients, families, and other hospice professionals that it is possible to shoulder the anxiety of intense mortality awareness, channeling the energy it creates into positive and productive outlets rather than displacing it in negative ways onto others. I know, therefore, that it is possible for human beings to live in ways that neither foster denial of death nor allow the anxiety of mortality awareness to poison the sphere of social relationships. The current interest among the more general public in issues of death and dying is a signal that we are not morally stagnant as a people.

Analyzing this same human predicament in a slightly different way, Robert J. Lifton[8] writes not so much about the psychological imperative to deny one's mortality (though he includes this in his analysis as an undeniable fact of the human psyche) but more of a need to encounter death with some sense of continuity with life. Whereas the starkest reading of Ernest Becker's analysis would lead to the conclusion that all immortality striving is bad, is the root of evil, Lifton distinguished between healthy and unhealthy immortality striving, seeking for what he called *symbolic immortality*. Meditating on the human encounter with the reality of death, Lifton wrote:

> While I cannot imagine my nonexistence, I can very well imagine a world in which *I* do not exist. That imaginative capacity is the basis for our theory of symbolic immortality. . . . While the denial of death is universal, the inner life-experience of a sense of immortality, rather than reflecting such denial, may well be the most authentic psychological alternative to that denial.[9]

Lifton then outlines modes in which a healthy sense of symbolic immortality may occur. The first is the *biological mode*, which focuses on family life and especially on children. The second is the *religious mode*, focused particularly on concepts of life after death. The third is the *creative mode*, in which focus is placed on aesthetic imagination and inventiveness. The fourth is the *mode of nature*, where focus centers on the human place in the transcending natural order. The fifth is the *mode of experiential transcendence*, by which Lifton means the sense of an intense and all-encompassing mystical union.

In examining Lifton's modes of symbolic immortality (to which other modes could be added) it becomes clear that there are healthy and unhealthy paths within each mode. Lifton's point is well-taken, however, that the universality of death denial does not leave us helpless puppets of those who would manipulate our unconscious narcissism, guilt, and sense of inadequacy. There are productive modes of living in which death anxiety is considerably eased, allowing us to place enough distance between our unconscious urges and our acting upon those unconscious urges to create a real space for moral and ethical living.

* * *

This points to the conclusion that even in a post-Christian era, people will seek pathways into authentic self-transcendence. And we have seen in the past decade or two, if anything, a revival of interest in religion and spirituality. The real question concerning the future of Christianity is not whether the spiritual interests of people can be kept enough alive for the religion to prosper. The real question is whether Christianity itself will be able to keep up with the burgeoning spiritual interest of the people. I suggest that the free church/believers church perspective is ideally suited to the post-Christian era, a time in which people seek authentic and transcending spiritual connections outside the commanding, authoritarian structures of institutional religion.

In an early work focused on the spirituality of the early Anabaptist movement, I outlined three major points that constitute the spiritual core that movement.[10] Here I want to look at these three points again in the context the emerging post-Christian context.

THE IMMEDIACY OF THE HUMAN RELATIONSHIP WITH GOD

In the sixteenth century, this sense that each person could establish a relationship with God directly, without the need for mediation, led to a criticism and rejection of special *places* (church buildings, shrines and pilgrimages), *persons* (saints, monks and priests), *times* (the church calendar) and *objects* (icons and relics) that in medieval European Christianity were thought necessary to mediate the relationship of people with God. In our time, these particular entities have been deconstructed sufficiently that we can freely experiment with including such elements in our spiritual lives. However, the central point remains that in the matters of spiritual living, no one stands taller than anyone else in the eyes of God. Spiritual authority can only be earned and freely given in the post-Christian era. When such authority is taken by force, insisting that it is necessary for mediating the human relationship with God, people will simply withdraw consent and 'vote with their feet,' as the saying goes.

Although many people are no doubt drawn to traditions that remove from their shoulders the need to work out their own salvation by telling them exactly what to believe and how to practice that belief (i.e., acting as institutional mediators between the people and their god) it is also true that large numbers of people in our society have come to value the sense of spiritual freedom and adventure made possible by the modern demise of religious authoritarianism. Such people are unlikely to abandon spiritual adventure to be part of the churches. They are likely to see the value of the Anabaptist-Mennonite view of the immediacy of the human relationship with God, a teaching that fosters the very spiritual freedom and adventure we have come to appreciate so deeply.

DISCIPLESHIP FOCUSED ON THE LIFE OF JESUS AS MODEL

Lately we have seen an astonishing rise in interest concerning the life of the historical Jesus of Nazareth. While few suggest we should or can live precisely like a Palestinian peasant of 2000 years ago, there is a pervasive sense that the life of active love that Jesus exemplified is profoundly relevant to the needs of our time. Granted that much of the surge in spiritual interest in general is much wider than deep, nevertheless there is a broad understanding that a deepening spirituality entails changes in the way one lives and in one's moral habits. People experiencing a deepening spiritual connection with the transcendent Divine feel themselves being moved toward gestures of love and compassion for others. There is a growing appreciation across a large spectrum of spiritual seekers that active love and nonviolence not only correspond to their spiritual leading, but are profoundly healing in a world sick with hatred and violence.

Yet even with a strong desire to love our neighbors, the world is very confusing. What is given to one is frequently taken from another. And so we very often stand there asking the age-old question, "Who is my neighbor?" Here I believe is the root of the current interest in looking to the life of Jesus as a model. For whatever else is said about him, it is clear that Jesus was able to express this active love and concern for those he met in a way his followers recognized as authentic.

Of course Jesus did not and could not have confronted many of the important moral and ethical issues we confront today. A question like, "What exactly is the nature of 'human life,' and when does it begin and end in the individual?" was simply not part of Jesus' vocabulary and would have made no sense in his time. Nevertheless, people do find that in coming closer to the life of Jesus, allowing that narrative to shape and influence their personal sense of life and its meaning, light is shed on a large spectrum of the moral and ethical issues we do confront. That this will continue to be the case is really what the future of the Christian religion will stand on in a post-Christian era.

THE CHRISTIAN LIFE AND FAITH
IS CORPORATE IN CHARACTER

The past 200 years have seen the rise of the cult of the individual in America. The increasingly dominant social philosophy has been one of *expressive individualism*. On the whole, this has been a good thing. Few of us would want to return to a time in which the individual had little or no choice concerning religion, profession, place, and marriage partner, not even to mention personal tastes and preferences in music, art, and other lifestyle areas. Even so, we have also become aware in recent decades that this single-minded pursuit of individual expression has many costs we had not fully appreciated. Freedom from the restraints of the village has progressed to the breakdown of a common sense of community. Freedom from arranged marriages has progressed to a sky-rocketing divorce rate and fleeting and unfulfilling serial relationships. Freedom to pursue our profession of choice has progressed to where work life is measured largely by dollar rewards. And in all of this, the individual is left alone and lonesome. It is little wonder, then, that the shine has tarnished on the philosophy of expressive individualism, and that people are beginning to look for social alternatives to the profound alienation our atomized individualism has brought.

The voluntarily gathered Christian community, as a *community of demonstration* of the gospel message, is one viable and potentially significant alternative source of personal meaning and value in face of the combined atomizing forces of individualism, technology, and self-centered capitalism. Awareness of the communal undercurrents of Christian spirituality is a driving force behind the current resurgence of interest in monastic mystical traditions and spiritual disciplines. It is within community that the process of disciplining life takes place, in recognition of the interdependency of each with the other. Our social venture into the wilds of expressive individualism has more than underlined for many of us the old dictum that no person stands alone as an island.

As said above, my hope is that the move into the post-Christian era will be grasped as a positive opportunity, not a fate to be feared. The spiritual tradition of the believers church appears ideally suited to this social environment. The immediacy of the human relationship with God establishes the free and voluntary character of Christian spiritual life. Recognition that Christian spiritual life is corporate in character connects that freedom to concrete responsibility to other flesh-and-blood human beings, potentially overcoming the profound alienation and loneliness of the modern ethos. Discipleship focused on the Jesus' life as a model of active love and nonviolence provides motivating direction for communal discernment and action, which in turn offers that context for decisions of daily living for each member of the community.

9

RESPONSES

WE MUST ALSO TALK ABOUT TRUTH

Daniel Liechty locates himself within the tradition of liberalism as a "post-liberal," that is, a liberal without the characteristically liberal optimism concerning the goodness of human beings and society. It may be helpful, briefly, to call to mind the liberal conception of religion. Friedrich Schleiermacher, the father of liberal theology, argued that the fountain of religion was the awareness of being absolutely dependent on something transcendental. In *The Christian Faith* (1835), he argued that all religious utterances (including doctrines and creeds) could be evaluated and reformulated in terms of how well they expressed the experience of absolute dependence. So the doctrines of creation, the divine attributes of God, the consciousness of sin in human beings, the consciousness of grace in Christ and in the story of salvation, could be understood as attempting to put words to that primary and primal experience.

Religious communities can then be understood as the communities within which a certain set of signs and practices have been accepted as normative. Consequently, all religions can be placed on a continuous hierarchy of how well a particular religion's set of signs and practices express the experience of dependence. For Schleiermacher, Christianity said it best.

Although it is not a systematic theology, Liechty's *Reflecting on Faith in a Post-Christian Time* can be understood as an updated version of *The Christian Faith*. And in that light, it is an important contribution to current theology. He argues along familiar liberal lines that there is a source of religion. In terms of the description of that source, he accepts the contribution of anthropologist Ernest Becker, who claims that responding to the terror of anticipating death is inescapably the most important human task. On Becker's analysis, human culture (broadly speaking) is a sophisticated network of signs and practices designed to help us cope in denying and accepting ways with the fact that we are fragile and vulnerable beings. Given this account, religion at its best helps us not to escape but rather to internalize and incorporate our awareness of our selves as being-toward-death.

The compelling aspect of the analysis is Liechty's "theory of generative mortality anxiety." According to this theory, the driving force behind evil is the flight from mortality. In an insightful and penetrating critique, Liechty shows how the human fight against evil brings even more evil into the world because evil is too narrowly defined and focused as it becomes identified with our human enemy. This understanding of evil is also theologically useful in that it provides a rule for reflection about God: we ought to be suspicious of conceptions of God that appear to justify demonizations of other human beings, and we ought to give privileged consideration to conceptions of God that lead us to reconcile with those from whom we have been alienated and have seen as Other. The resultant hierarchy of conceptions of God is thus very like Schleiermacher's.

Liechty refrains from talking in terms of truth concerning our reflections of God and this creates a problem. If we do refrain from using the language of truth, what controls do we have to safeguard us against the objection that although we have now arrived at a better and purer conception of God, at the end of the day we are left with "merely" human projection? He might respond that using the language of truth will not solve that problem for us. After three hundred fifty years, modern philosophy has now reached the consensus that the search for truth ought to be abandoned because the human mind is incapable of grasping reality—earthly or divine—and that instead we ought to restrict the vocabulary of our judgments about conceptions of the world to words such as helpful, useful, and adequate.

But Christians cannot afford to accept this conclusion about the human mind. We, and here I mean all of us who are interested in religious matters, ought to have the courage to engage in the quest for truth (again) in matters transcendent. We can't, of course, peel back the curtain of the universe to see who and what God really is, but just as it is not possible for the grass to be green and orange at the same time, so the Christian, the Hindu, and the atheist conceptions of the transcendent cannot all be true.

What tools of discovery do we then have? I suggest that we have each other! In *Three Rival Versions of Moral Enquiry* (1990), Alasdair MacIntyre shows that it is possible to engage in dialogue with adherents of other traditions of inquiry such that we might come to discover internal inconsistencies within our own tradition or that of our dialogue partners. This discovery of limitations would in turn give us reasons to reformulate our understanding of God or to adopt another religion's understanding of God if it becomes apparent that it is superior. Such a reformulation is unintelligible unless it is understood as a movement toward truth. It seems to miss the point at the end of the day to say, "That was a helpful construction of God." Surely there is more to the human quest than merely constructing useful conceptions of God; surely the point of the quest is that we deeply want to understand God rightly.

Liechty's concern with applying the language of truth is the abuse that claims to truth historically have legitimated. In wanting to undermine that legitimation, Liechty fails to consider the alternative that the quest for truth can be—and ought to be—disassociated from discussions of salvation. For example, Christians would want to say that Abram, a Semite from ancient Ur, clearly did not understand God in the same way that Christians do now, and yet he still had meaningful experiences of God. Experiencing God and understanding God are not the same. Therefore it is at least logically possible to argue that while all religions are engaged in experiencing and understanding God, only one religion understands God rightly. And if there is such a thing as the source of religion, surely this is it: the desire to know the God whom we have experienced in our lives.

—*Christian Early, Harrisonburg, Virginia, Associate Professor of Philosophy and Theology, Eastern Mennonite University*

DOES IT HAVE STAYING POWER?

This book is entitled *Reflecting on Faith in a Post-Christian Time*, but it is not much revised from its 1990 publication under the title *Theology in Postliberal Perspective*. Liechty states in the introduction that it is written for a "professional lay audience." If so, it should, I think, have given more attention to explicating theological and biblical terms that are the verbal currency used by people in Christian churches and in the Christian tradition generally, terms such as atonement, justification, the kingdom of God, the deity and humanity of Christ, and the doctrine of the Trinity. We may notice especially the absence of a treatment of the cross, a central theme in the New Testament and in historic Christian theology.

I do consider the last part of chapter 2, apart from the Ernest Becker theory, a superb and insightful description of the human problem: sin. Too few Christians recognize the "ambiguity of evil. We commit our most evil acts out of heroic intentions, the very desire to eradicate evil." Liechty here writes of "military generals and public executioners [who] always see themselves as working toward the good on both sides of any conflict" (p. 47). He could have included any and all of us in this description.

I question whether Liechty should give as much weight as he does to Ernest Becker's theory about the fear of mortality as the dominating concern of human existence and therefore the clue to understanding all religion, including the Christian religion. "God is our highest immortality symbol," says Liechty (p. 52). Was it the fear of mortality that drove Jesus? Beginning on page 108, the author similarly goes on for over a page on a Peter Munz theory that "may help us understand what might have been involved" in Christianity becoming "the major religion of the Roman world," a theory about a "male/creationist" versus a "female/ emanental myth of origins."

It is a temptation to get enamored with some current theory or philosophy. Thomas Aquinas got enchanted with and hitched his theology to Aristotle. This past century Bultmann and McQuarrie hitched their theologies to Heidegger's existentialism. Such theologies become passé (even if they ever were genuinely useful) when the philosophies they adopted are left behind.

I agree with Liechty's Excursive Update at the end of chapter 4, in which he deplores Mennonite theologians' uncritical endorsement of the traditional formulations of the doctrine of the Trinity as an important and even indispensable doctrine without clarifying what it really means or should mean. One Mennonite theologian admits that this "dogma" (Liechty's term) is an "obscure, speculative, and controversial notion" and yet considers it important (p. 82). Unfortunately Liechty too doesn't clarify what it should mean. Given the emphasis the doctrine of the Trinity has been given in Christian history, this is an important and urgent task, especially in the light of Christianity's encounter today with Islam's stark monotheism.

Liechty deserves commendation for including a chapter on what one could loosely call the relationship of Christian faith to other faiths. In liberal circles in might be labeled inter-religious dialogue, in conservative circles the question of missions and evangelism, the missionary imperative. This is a subject deserving attention in our increasingly pluralist world today, and more and more theologians are addressing it. Liechty weighs in on the side of a Mennonite Central Committee kind of style—that is, that the Christian witness expresses itself in deeds of service and that this is the really only appropriate way for Christianity to commend itself to others. He is very hesitant to invite conversions, instead opting for "helping people along the continuum of social maturity" (p. 128) within their own religious traditions.

Here Liechty may have a point, especially in light of the fact that so much of evangelism and mission has been an exercise in spraying the world with empty clichés. Or worse. As Liechty asks, "Can one still find salvation in Christ" after a history of "Christian" discrimination, oppression, and "economic and cultural imperialism"? (p. 93). In light of this I would, however, call for more rather than less verbal clarification by serious followers of Jesus about what faith in him means. I think I am as aware as Liechty of the magnitude of the task required in making this corrective, of clarifying the real meaning of the message of Jesus. But we can still share with the apostle Paul a profound confidence in the power of this good news about Jesus, rightly proclaimed, to transform lives and reshape societies.

Let me here invoke an observation from Gordon Kaufman's *God, Mystery, Diversity*: that over the centuries faiths shape societies. In light of that we can see what people today are saying with their feet despite the evils of Constantinian Christianity. Migrations still seem to be in the direction of countries shaped by the Christian tradition. I want, however, to be as Anabaptist as Liechty in pushing for a de-Constantinianized Christianity and for a recovery of a New Testament Jesus.

Most Christian readers will have the biggest objection to Liechty's view that ideas of God are projections of the human imagination: "Undeniably, the very idea of God is projective wish fulfillment" (p. 63). This theology is associated most commonly with the name of Ludwig Feuerbach, German philosopher of the 1800s, though Liechty does not mention Feuerbach. Liechty speaks of transcendence, to be sure, but that is self-transcendence, not encounter with a transcendent reality. In his claim that theology is a work of constructing an adequate image of God, Liechty may be thought to be following Gordon Kaufman, who also uses the language of imaginative construction of concepts of God. But if I am not mistaken, Kaufman still holds that our constructions are of something that is actually there, something that we encounter and that encounters us, which Kaufman calls "mystery."

One can't help asking whether a theology premised on the claim that the idea of God is wish fulfillment has staying power. Won't such a theology almost inevitably break down? The next step often seems to run along these lines: Let's be honest! If belief in God is wish fulfillment, people of integrity have the strength and courage to face the truth and simply dismiss any belief in God in favor of a robust humanism.

Liechty's essay may be speaking for more Mennonites and other postmodern Christians than we might like to admit. They, like Liechty, have undergone a serious reconstruction of their faith (or even erosion, some would call it), thanks perhaps to modern science or the secular mood of our times. Yet this cohort of people retains a powerful attachment to the figure of Jesus, to Jesus' pacifism and other radical teachings, and to the community of the church, an attachment that is more than nostalgia for Mennonite or other similar Christian roots. Too many Mennonites have felt that their traditional theology, too much influenced by fundamentalism, requires one to "place one's intellect in a safe deposit box" (footnote 8 to chap. 3). Well said. People want and deserve theological honesty.

What is Liechty's warrant or justification for holding to his (what I would call) minimalist but tenacious faith? He is right, I think, in admitting that there is no objective proof of the rightness of the Jesus way, of the claim that this way is the way to our true humanity. In this respect postmodernism is not far from historic Christian doctrine, as J. Denny Weaver has also argued. As John Calvin puts it, there is no proof of the truth of Christianity other than the inner persuasion of the word of God and the Holy Spirit. With faith it is not like the television shows where the right answer is confirmed by some audible "ding"! Or, as William

James puts it more poetically, there is no cosmic bell that tolls when the truth is in. God doesn't provide some unmistakable supernatural verification to show who possesses the truth, for then faith would no longer be faith, a voluntary commitment, but intellectual coercion.

So there is little point to argument over deficiencies in Liechty's theology. But always room for dialogue, such as the one begun here. It befits those of us interested in preserving what we would consider a more traditional or at least more biblical theology to demonstrate its truth by its fruits and not just by intellectual coherence, which in too much of historic orthodoxy and modern fundamentalism has been devoid of ethical fruit and thus shown to be hollow. Answers to Liechty will need to match his concern, and even passion, for ethical life.

I am reminded, however, of a well-known quote from the late Elton Trueblood, Quaker theologian and professor at Earlham School of Religion. Trueblood once wrote about "cut-flower ethics," by which he meant ethical conduct that continues for some time even though cut off from its spiritual roots. But cut off from its roots it eventually withers. We will need to leave it to time to tell whether the ethical commitment of Liechty's theology has the power to produce and sustain an ethical community on the model of Jesus or whether such an ethic needs the roots of a more biblical faith.

—*Marlin Jeschke, Goshen, Indiana, Professor Emeritus of Philosophy and Religion, Goshen College*

WE NEED A STRONGER GOD

Here is our reality: we live in a thoroughly pluralistic society where it seems there are many paths to God. More reality: the history of the Christian church is splattered with the blood of innocent people. Horrible atrocities have been committed in the name of God. We as Christians have been more than intolerant. We have killed people in the name of Jesus. There must be another way to God than the way of intolerance and arrogance, the way of slaughter and plunder.

That's our reality. But Liechty's answer to that reality—embracing a religious pluralism which has as its highest values pacifism, inclusivity, and freedom—falls short of the mark. All those things are wonderful and hopefully part of everyone's religious experience, but one needs a power higher than oneself to live by these high standards. One needs to recognize sin as more than just an anxious reaction to death. Somehow, somewhere, we must be transformed by a power larger than we are, a power that is divine, in order for us to be free from the powers that make us warlike, exclusivist, and tied in sinful knots.

Perhaps the divine being is One who is bigger than the Christian God, and I am open to that possibility (although that begins to go beyond the purpose of my response to this book). But Liechty, by his analysis of sin and by his Christology, leaves us basically with ourselves and our own human strivings to do these good things. That, for me, is too close to humanism, one of those old modern horses that died awhile back.

Liechty uses Becker's theory of death anxiety as one of the frames for our post-Christian discussion. Becker explains the root of sin as our fear of death. We know we are going to die, yet we have a strong urge to live, which creates enormous anxiety for us. We repress this anxiety by creating and giving allegiance to symbols of immortality as a way to deal with the tension and fear.

While the threat of death can be a strong motivator for behavior, the biblical narrative would point to another root cause and origin of sin. In the mythic story of Adam and Eve, the couple sins before facing the threat of death. They see the fruit and are persuaded by the serpent that indeed it may be eaten, even though God says otherwise. The fruit is tempting because, upon consumption, it will open their eyes and make them like God. The primary motivation for sin, then, is not death, but a desire to be God or to become wise (Gen. 3:6). And the temptation to sin comes not only from interior forces—their own desire and pride—but also from the outside—the serpent. Death comes as a result of disobedience.

The other Fall etiologies strike complementary notes. The Tower of Babel is another clear attempt to be God, as the people build a tower to reach the heavens and make a name for themselves. Cain killing Abel and the wickedness of Noah's day show a variation of trying to be God—the taking of lives. Murder and war—two of the most potent immortality symbols for Liechty— are also two of the most destructive ways we try to usurp the Divinity (Otherness?) of God. Did the people in Genesis 11 desire to build the tower because they knew they would die? Possibly. Did Cain kill Abel because of his own repressed fear of dying? Again that was probably part of it. But the Fall stories point to a problem that goes beyond that. The ancient Hebrews understood death not as the cause of sin as its most terrifying result.

If we could, through medical breakthroughs, kill death (destroy death's grip on us—is that better?), would that take sin away from this world? Would we then become better people? Would we stop being greedy and arrogant?

Ironically, the very thing Adam and Eve try to do—grab for divinity—is the thing Jesus does not do, according to Philippians 2:6-11. What might that mean? The ancient hymn loses much of its force if Jesus really had no divinity to grasp (granted that some scholars do read the Greek that way). Likewise, Jesus' refusal to use force, loses much of its power if he's just a poor Gallilean who had no other options anyway.

Jesus is not divine, according to Liechty, for the primary reason that his deification has led Christians away from the concept of God as essentially nonviolent. The early church, he says, mistakenly made Jesus divine as a survival tool. Yet this same church, for the first 300 years, was essentially pacifistic. If Jesus as Lord created a barrier for pacifism, inclusivity, and freedom for all, then the early church was very effective at overcoming this barrier.

I don't believe that the affirmation "Jesus is Lord" caused the intolerance and violence as much as did a basic misunderstanding of this Lordship. Starting with Constantine, Christians chose to use unjust means to reach a "Christian" end. But Jesus, following in the tradition of the God of the Hebrews, chose not to force his way—ever. The end never justified the means.

Jesus is like the God who allowed the Israelites at Shechem to choose this day whom they would serve, after all the grace and rescue that had been poured out for them. Jesus lived in such as way that no one was ever coerced into following him. The temptations in the wilderness, his reluctance to have word spread about his miracles, and his execution demonstrate for us what true nonviolence, inclusivity and freedom are. And in that way, we are to be just like Jesus.

Liechty is right that nonviolent love, pacifism, is all-important. Jesus' nonviolent, complete obedience to God that led to the cross is exactly what did defeat evil. Jesus did not capitulate to the fear of torture and death, and in that way defeated evil. There was nothing worse they could do to him. He won. Jesus defeated oppression because of how he defeated death. If we can embrace that same strategy for defeating evil (trusting God for the outcome or future), then we too can overcome it.

But the question remains. Do I have the guts to go to the cross without believing in some divine presence? Do I have the guts to live out enemy love without the hope of resurrection? Or maybe, do we sin by wrongly grasping divinity, when we believe that somehow we can seek God within ourselves and that will be enough? According to the biblical narrative, Jesus didn't just have to accept his mortality. Jesus became Lord, not only over the principalities and powers of the rulers in Jerusalem, but also over all the powers—even death. Without resurrection, Jesus is a tragedy because the powers won.

Can Jesus be Lord without Christians using this theological understanding to sanction oppression? Yes, some Anabaptist ancestors lived out that reality. To take it a step farther, is it needful for Jesus to be Lord for us to be pacifists, and live in life-affirming ways? Well, no. Many people who practice other religions are pacifists and live exemplary lives. It would seem, however, that for people to live out the extreme demands of enemy love that some divine Other must be Lord for them.

If it is true that sin comes to us from outside sources as well as from within and that it produces death and not the other way around, then we need a stronger antidote than just accepting our mortality. We need divine help, and not just from an immortality symbol we call God. "Choose you this day whom you will serve" is different than "Choose this day which God you will construct and it will be so." We need—resurrection. Liechty is right about the great power of the immortality symbols. These potentially good things can and almost always do become fetishes. They take on a god-like power. We need, therefore, a strong God who frees us from sin, including our fear of death, and gives us the power we need to do what is otherwise impossible.

—*Michele Hershberger, Chair of the Bible Department and Associate Professor, Hesston (Kan.) College*

THE AUTHORITY OF COURAGE AND HONESTY

Soren Kierkegaard repeatedly confessed that he had no authority to preach; one can only imagine how much less credible he would have been if he claimed instead with equal frequency that he *did* have authority to preach! Daniel Liechty's voice in these pages struck me with an extraordinary ring of authority,

perhaps akin to the Dane's: persuasive because he is not shout-
ing to persuade, instructive because he is not pushing to instruct,
delightful because he is not striving to delight. Rather, what he *is*
trying to do is simply *to reflect*, to think honestly on paper, to con-
solidate in "a work" (or "an attempt"—an essay) his own personal musings and readings and reasonings and intuitions. This
honesty carries a most precious authority, by helping this reader
at least "find . . . new ways of perceiving [my] world of experience" (21).

To read reflections like these is for me like experiencing hospitality. One is invited to make oneself at home in someone else's
internal world. I found this world wonderfully hospitable. I left
my stay with Liechty stimulated, challenged, enriched.

So this book strikes me not so much as a work of polemics or
even scholarship but as an artifact, an artifact of a sincere spiritually alive person, an artistic composition by a human being trying to grapple honestly and humbly and wisely with the myster-
ies and complexities and paradoxes of life, just as a song might
grapple with joy (in a Celtic jig or reel) or disappointment (the
blues) or glory (a hymn) or mystery (in a simple Appalachian
melody).

Some of my friends, I think, will like this book less than I do.
They'll be troubled that Daniel presents himself both as believer
and atheist (what!), and that he questions traditional orthodox
trinitarianism (82) and traditional orthodox Christology (87), for
starters. But I hope many of my friends will withhold judgment
and read these reflections despite what they find troubling.

Why? I think Liechty will give even unsympathetic readers
an insight into what it feels like for a "postmodern person" to
seek to be

- true—which requires expressing one's doubts honestly;
- faithful—which may include breaking faith with orthodoxies if those orthodoxies seem inescapably unethical or
  unworthy of God; and
- moral—which generally brings one out of the either-or
  world of theory and into the millions of colors (as some
  computer graphics settings put it) and shadowy world of
  experience.

It's important for people who do not identify with postmodern (or post-Christian, or post-whatever) culture to understand
those like Liechty who do, if for no other reason than because

their children and grandchildren, not to mention their neighbors, may find themselves walking the same trail.

I have found in my experience that there is a peculiar and agonizing stretch of the westward trail lying in a valley between the plateau of high modernity and the foothills of postmodernity. In this treacherous valley, one is in the shadow of modern rationalistic skepticism from sunrise until about 11:58 a.m., and in the shadow of postmodern ambiguity and ambivalence from about 12:02 p.m. until sunset. Clarity and light seem rare and short-lived. In the morning shadows, one is haunted by questions about certainty and uncertainty. In the afternoon shadows, one is haunted by questions of power and powerlessness. So it never gets very bright on this leg of the journey for very long. I sometimes compare it to wearing two pairs of sunglasses whose polarizations are askew, so that barely any light gets through.

Between writing the previous paragraph and completing the next, I have talked with three pastors walking in this dimness, each on the verge of losing faith. Three times I saw eyes brim with tears, eyes turn away and down, eyes close in an unspoken pain. These good Christian people would each benefit greatly from spending time in the hospitable inner world of a person who has walked this hard road and, having had his childhood faith thoroughly deconstructed, is now in the process of reconstructing it.

Liechty can help them because his eyes have adjusted to seeing as well as one can see in the dim light of this difficult stretch of the pathway. Those who have never walked in that valley will find it easy to criticize because of how much he has left behind. Those who have walked that valley will applaud gratefully for how much he has managed to salvage and retain.

For example, we'll applaud Liechty for grappling with the body/mind bifurcation we in the West have inherited at least twice, first from Platonism and later from Descartes (39). The "nonreductive physicalism" he advocates is important because it takes seriously findings from many fields of modern science (evolutionary biology, psychopharmacology, neurobiology) while taking seriously—and resisting—the reductionism that so often infuses interpretations of those findings.

We'll also applaud Liechty for calling us to "take a stand of unbelief" with regard to to the false gods of power and consumption. We'll thank him for challenging us not to confuse human empires with our eschatological hope.

Likewise, we'll applaud Liechty for tackling the tough subject of religious pluralism while refusing to take any of the easy exits or short cuts veering off to the left or the right of the path. We'll applaud because he reminds us that our beliefs lead to behavior, and because he asserts that unethical, destructive, unloving behavior is a good reason to question the truth of all beliefs that foster that behavior.

True, there may have been occasions where some of us would wish for Liechty to speak the language of the faith community, not just the language of the social science community. Terms like *social maturity* and *inclusive freedom*, for example, both gain and lose something for us when they replace the word *love*. But maybe we in the faith community have become so familiar with our own lexicon—love, truth, grace, redemption—that we don't really know what we mean when we jabber on and on, so being challenged by a foreign lexicon is good for us.

Reading Liechty's book, I kept thinking of the biblical book of Ecclesiastes. The questioning sage has an honored place in our Judeo-Christian community of faith: the reflections of the sage are not excluded from the library of Scripture because they question and disturb. No, they are included to remind us that it takes as much courage to face hostile ideas and dangerous questions with honesty as it does to face hungry lions or violent giants or capricious kings. Perhaps that courage and honesty are the real source of Liechty's authority. For those who aren't themselves asking the questions Liechty has faced, this book will disturb. For those have are asking the tough questions of modernity and postmodernity, the book will bring comfort and encouragement.

—*Brian McLaren, Laurel, Maryland, is a pastor, (www.crcc.org); author of* A New Kind of Christian, Finding Faith, The Story We Find Ourselves In, *and more; and senior fellow in emergent (www.emergentvillage.com)*

DANIEL LIECHTY RESPONDS

I want to thank each of the people who responded to this essay for their thoughtful comments, including Professor Friesen for his insightful Foreword as well as Michael King, who in his Series Editor's Preface masterfully sets the stage for real dialogue to occur. In the comments following, my intention is to move this discussion forward, not to joust intellectually or to show off rhetorical skills of argumentation. I would not want ending this book on notes of controversy to skew much more comprehensive areas of agreement. I am thankful for the affirmations these brothers and sisters have given for the experimental reflections I offer in this book and also for their ability to keenly zero in on salient points where need for clarification occurs. At the risk of simply repeating what I wrote in the body of the essay, I will try to address myself more clearly to a few of these points directly, as space allows.

The reality of God? A number of the responses seem to assume that I portray Godself only as a human, social, and psychological projection. This is not ultimately my intention, though I do think that our human conceptions of God inevitably include projection. My intention is to sharply raise the point that, given our human finiteness, we are not in a position to answer questions about Godself. We affirm the existence of a God who is there on the basis of faith alone. Every person who does his or her thinking in the context of the contemporary world has at least tentatively entertained the frightful hypothesis that there is no God, that our existence is a matter of the random chance formations of matter and energy, and that we are radically alone in the cosmos. There is no grand-slam, definitive disproof of this hypothesis, which is perhaps even more disconcerting.

This terrifying vision of radical aloneness in the universe is the inescapable background noise for serious reflection on human life and its meaning and possibility in the world. Our embrace of a God who is there is a wager of faith and does not itself change the material circumstances of the world in which we live. The more loudly we proclaim our faith, in desperate need to drown out this background noise, the more we are reminded of the Bard's quote, "Methinks thou doest protest too much!" Our faith itself becomes exposed as an expression of anxiety, the root of which is our anxiety concerning mortality (symbolized here as cosmic meaninglessness, nothingness, the Void.)

Acceptance and honest acknowledgment of this terrifying hypothesis as the unavoidable background noise of the human condition does not mean, however, that the hypothesis is true. The movement away from meaninglessness, nothingness, the Void, and toward that which offers us a firm sense of conviction, purpose, and significance, is also an undeniable, inescapable, and critical aspect of what it means to be human. The premature embrace of the "null hypothesis" is itself a response born of anxiety, a claim to know that which we simply cannot know (a claim, in effect, to be "more than human.")

Of course, our religious faith is bolstered by personal experience, by close fellowship with others who also embrace our faith, by studying and repeating to ourselves the historical and contemporary narratives that support our faith. The thicker and more interlocking, interwoven, this narrative, the more convincing it becomes and the less susceptible to collapse under the weight of circumstances. But a strong and honest faith cannot be separated from honest and ongoing doubt—a heartfelt and not simply rhetorical recognition that, after all, we might be wrong. Without that, our faith becomes potentially dangerous. We certainly do not lack for illustrative examples of this in the history of Christianity, other faiths, the political and social world in which we live, nor even in our own individual lives.

My intention, therefore, is not to claim to know something about Godself that is beyond the ken of a mortal being to know. It is rather to spotlight how essential it is for us to become more open and embracing of honest doubt—the simple admission that, after all, we might be wrong—as a real and necessary component of our faith, despite the fact that this admittedly undermines our sense of absolute certainty about our faith and exposes us to the very anxiety from which religious faith functions to shield us.

Strong faith and honest doubt are partners, not oppositions, through which we are then enabled to become much more open to those of other experiences of faith, and much less prone to that urge (again, born of anxiety) to conquer (even symbolically, emotionally, intellectually) any opposing beliefs. A strong faith is paradoxically further strengthen by the dynamic movement of honest doubt, recognition of limitation, the embrace of ambiguity. As I understand it, the need to lay claim to absolute certainty, while undeniably a central human passion and more than pleasing to the crowd, is a signal of faith's weakness, not her robust strength. But then again, I might be wrong.

Trinity? I am apparently understood as denying or opposing the doctrine of the Trinity. This is also not my intention. I am not saying the church was in error in its trinitarian formulations. In fact, I offer a sympathetic account of how this process might have come about historically—as a powerful antidote to the claim that *Caesar is Lord/God*. I do mean to suggest, however, that there was error afoot (an historical wrong turn, if we can call it that) when the church claimed the trinitarian model as the *sine qua non* of Christian belief and began excluding and persecuting anyone who found other models of God more meaningful in their lives.

We largely continue in that historical wrong turn today. We would be poorer for it were there no more attempts to construct trinitarian models of God. I find some of these constructs (Gordon Kaufman's work, for example) to be very useful, thought-provoking, and edifying. In short, good stuff! But there are also nontrinitarian models of God that are useful, thought-provoking, and edifying. We do ourselves a disservice by confining ourselves only to trinitarian models. This disservice occurs not only because we limit ourselves intellectually, emotionally, and spiritually to trinitarian explorations of God, but also because we exclude ourselves from close fellowship with others who embrace other models. I would like to see a hundred flowers bloom in our thinking about God, which would certainly include trinitarian models for thinking about God.

Finally, I want especially to thank Brian McLaren for his use of musical metaphor in his encounter with this piece of writing. As I read that, my heart leaped, and I said, "Yes! He really understands what I am doing here!" Psychoanalysts tell us that we want to be both loved and understood, but push comes to shove, people will choose being really understood over being loved. Reading McLaren, I can testify there is a firm conveyance of love, Eros and Agapé, in knowing one has been deeply understood.

QUESTIONS TO HELP
GUIDE STUDY AND DISCUSSION

1. Studying the chart on page 157, how many of "ways of being religious" can you identify in the schools of thought in your own religion? What do you think are the more and less important themes in North American Christianity? Among Mennonites? Among your particular congregation?

2. As we become adults, we outgrow ideas of God we held as children. Yet out adult ideas of God (as well as most other crucial concepts) often contain and are shaped by the ideas we held as children. Reflecting on the earliest ideas of God you remember, list two or three of the most important characteristics of God you held as a child. Discuss similarities and differences between these early notions and your adult understanding of God.

3. Many children picture God in the form of a real human authority figure, such as parent, grandparent, teacher, minister, or elderly person in their local community. Try to remember the faces of those who represented God to you at different stages in your life. What common threads do you see in these faces? What in your face might represent God to your young children, nieces and nephews, or other children in your congregation?

4. Imagine a friend recently came out of a coma after a brain injury. Current sensory functions and short-term memory are intact but long-term memory is lost, including memories connected with the meaning of religious terms. You discuss your faith with your friend. But when you try to explain one term, you find yourself using three or four others your friends does not recognize. What would be your starting point for communicating with your friend what is central to your faith? In other words, what are the most simple terms in which you can express

your faith and by which the more abstract meanings are built up? Role play this with a group if you have opportunity.

5. Reflecting back on one or two crucial and emotionally laden events in your life (for example, recovery from a serious illness or accident, leaving home, becoming a parent, the death of a close loved one) have you noticed subtle or dramatic changes in your understanding of who God is subsequent to these events? What changes have occurred?

6. Christian faith affirms that Jesus of Nazareth was human in every way. Yet, except for the final hours or so of his life, most Christians have real trouble, may even feel it sacrilegious, picturing Jesus in the most human situations pertaining to a vulnerable and mortal human body—situations such as experiencing the diarrheic cramps and vomiting of a stomach virus, a badly bleeding cut, coping with adolescent sexual passion, having decaying teeth, allergic reactions to the environment. Should this be troubling? If Jesus were portrayed artistically as experiencing such suffering, would you find it sacrilegious? Why or why not?

7. Robert J. Lifton (p. 134) outlines at least five modes through which a healthy sense of symbolic immortality might be achieved. Do you lean toward one or more modes? Comparing Lifton's modes of symbolic immortality to the chart on ways of being religious (p. 157) what modes of symbolic immortality seem to correspond best with each of the ways of being religious?

8. The author focuses on three core values (pp. 135-137) comprising the spiritual energy that motivates an Anabaptist interpretation of faith: 1) the immediacy of the human relationship with God; 2) discipleship focused on the life of Jesus as model; and 3) the Christian life and faith is corporate in character.

In his monumental 1943 essay, "The Anabaptist Vision," Harold S. Bender also listed three core Anabaptist values: 1) "First and fundamental in the Anabaptist vision was the conception of the essence of Christianity as discipleship." 2) "A new concept of the church was created by the central principle of newness of life and applied Christianity." 3) "The third great element . . . was the ethic of love and nonresistance as applied to all human relationships" (http://w3.ime.net/~wchesley/anabaptist/anavis.html).

What similarities and differences do you see between these two attempts to articulate the core motivating values of the Anabaptist faith? What changes would you make to fit the statements more closely to your own faith?

APPENDIX 1: EIGHT WAYS OF BEING RELIGIOUS

	A) The Problem	B) The Answer	C) Individual Appropriation	D) Expressed Socially
Personal Experience of the Holy	sin, pride, pretension; incapacity, imperfection, imperfect functioning; separation from God	All-sufficiency of God (Absolute Other); Divine Surprise (Gift), uncontrollable, not programmed; "wakan" "mana" "maxpe"	nonverbal feeling, not intellectual; personal (inner) experience; submission, obedience, dependency, trust, faith, conversion	people demonstrate confidence, capacity; change of behavior; exuberance
Creation of Community Through Myth and Ritual	the power of chaos; willful alienation; sin and/or ignorance	Power of Divine Creation; transcendent creative activity; reconciliation to the Real (grace)	symbolic re-enactment of transcendent creative acts; reconciliation to the Real through Power of Grace	dependency on sacred mediators (priests), times (holy days) places (temples, holy lands); communal rituals
Daily Living That Expresses the Cosmic Law	social and cosmic disharmony (with cosmic law and cosmic relations) immature human beings; isolated, inauthentic	following the natural, cosmic, eternal, transcendent law; eternal harmony manifested in right social order	cultivating true self and proper self-identity through right social relations (morality, ethics); human existence part of divine order	culture and everyday activities reflect knowledge of eternal order; wisdom for orderly living based on ancient truth
Spiritual Freedom Through Discipline (Mysticism)	bondage to self; ignorance of separation from the Real	Transcendent Reality; knowledge of Godself; transcendent consciousness	personal discipline; inner realization and appropriation of immanent Reality; illumination of transcendent consciousness	detachment from social life; individual training from enlightened Masters
Achieving an Integrated Self Through Creative Interaction	loneliness; alienation; loss of identity; experience of depersonalization; insincerity	love, trust, concern; relatedness; personal integrity; depth in interpersonal relationships	attention to immediate responses to others; delight in human relationships; growth in acceptance of self and others	mental health concerns; group therapy; anti-institutionalism; social education for understanding of social deviance
Social and Economic Justice as an Ultimate Concern	inhumanity of the status quo and social-political institutions; injustice, inequality; failure to recognize human rights	justice in social relations; rapid social reform; universal capacity for moral integrity; innate human right to economic welfare	vision of and commitment to implement a just society; responsiveness to human needs	decisions made through rational discussion; social action to implement moral decisions; formation of just social institutions
New Life Through Technocracy	chaos and confusion; ignorance of basic facts about human existence; inability to control the environment; biological death	comfort and security; extending human lifespan; efficiency and order; technical control; truth as explicit, concise, precise, universal, objective	attention to empirical regularities; quest for objectivity; pragmatic theory of truth; suspicion of the intuitive; subordination to team effort	social commitment to this-world utopia; institutionalization of technology
Creating the Full Life Through Sensuous and Artistic Experience	abstractions; insensitivity to sensuous form; lack of feeling; lifelessness, sterility, lack of imagination	the power of sensuous experience; priority of aesthetic reality; creative imagination	intense attention to sensuous experience and perception; spontaneity, direct and vivid experience as 'moment of truth'	indifference to social convention; antirationalism; gatherings for mutual encouragement; advocacy of sensuality

Source: Streng, Lloyd and Allen 1973 (slightly modified)

APPENDIX 2

PACIFISM POST-9/11—THOUGHTS ON RESPONSIBLE CITIZENSHIP IN CONTEXT OF PLURALISTIC DEMOCRACY

*L*ike many Mennonites of my generation, my general sense of politics and pacifism has been shaped by specific spiritual and intellectual influences, experienced and reflected on in the context of particular events. Those spiritual and intellectual influences that stand out most clearly in my mind are Harold Bender's presentation of the Anabaptist Vision, as further interpreted through Guy F. Hershberger's understanding of nonresistance, and as mediated to me more directly through high school, college, and seminary classes with Harvey Yoder, Willard Swartley, J. Richard Burkholder, and John Howard Yoder.

Those of my generation reflected on these ideas in the context of the United States civil rights and anticolonialist, liberationist, and "power" movements of the 1960s and 1970s; the rise and fall of the American and European New Left; the Vietnam War, perceived as an American generational ritual of child sacrifice; and the general irrationality of Cold War "defense" politics, symbolized especially by a nuclear arms race in which an ability to bounce the rubble twenty times over compelled the other side to seek a security holy grail of twenty-one bounce capability.

In the atmosphere of Vietnam-style hot war and mutually assured destruction cold war, the traditional Mennonite interpretation of pacifist nonresistance, built on a firm foundation of a two-kingdoms theology, possessed strongly intuitive credibility. That there is a realm of violence running according to fundamentally and inherently different principles than a realm of nonviolence seemed to be an objective exegesis of the nightly Cronkite CBS report. ("And that's the way it is. . . . ") One hardly needed Mennonite theology to recognize this; it was a countercultural commonplace. The spirit of this perspective was caught very nicely, for example, in the Simon and Garfunkel anthem, "Silent Night/Six O'Clock News."

In retrospect, there was an emotionally and spiritually satisfying element to an interpretation that allowed such a clear and clean distinction between the Good Guys and the Bad Guys, with us as Good Guys standing firmly with God and Jesus. At the same time, the historical pessimism inherent in this general view was inadequate as a guide to political action in areas of concern other than overt militarism and violence. It too easily passed over the importance of civil rights work, social justice work such as union organizing, environmental activism, and many other areas in which significant numbers of young Mennonites of my generation—animated by our faith, to be sure, but also by the general generational Zeitgeist of optimism about social possibilities—found ourselves yearning to connect to wider movements of political and social change.

Our overwhelming embrace of the "politics of Jesus" was perhaps rooted less in deep understanding of the hermeneutical and theological nuances of John H. Yoder's reading of various New Testament texts, and more in a relatively facile intuition that this view justified political action on behalf of peace and social justice and reconciled such action with Anabaptist-Mennonite ideology. This then allowed us to be involved politically, yet somehow retain the sense of purity given us in the more traditional Mennonite view. At least I know that is how it was for me.

During the last several decades, my religious and theological views have been deconstructed and reconstructed several times. In relation to the place of peacemaking and politics, I have been strongly influenced by a serious reappropriation of Reinhold Niebuhr and a much more fundamental appreciation for theory corresponding to current understandings in the social sciences rather than only or primarily theology.

It is said that the events of September 11 may well be the formative event for the generation coming of age as the planes hit that Vietnam and the Cold War were for us Baby Boomers. Vietnam and the Cold War demonstrated to many Boomers the clay feet of the "ethical realists," as we watched those middle-aged, once left-leaning Christian socialists line up to bless America's every Cold War move. There seemed nothing that could not be baptized so long as motivated by anticommunism. Watching now as many once left-leaning, middle-aged Boomers wrap themselves in the flag of patriotism, competing to outdo each other in terms of what they will countenance in the name of a "war" on terrorism, I can't help but wonder what feet of clay we may be demonstrating to our youngers.

How post-September 11 events will shape the political consciousness of the current generation of young people, including Mennonites, remains to be seen. We may also assume that these events and reaction to them are different for U.S. citizens and citizens of other nation-states. I reflect here as a U.S. citizen, that is, as a citizen of a liberal, pluralistic, and democratic nation.

For those of my generation, the terrorist attacks certainly strain pacifist logic and commitment to the maximum. Historically, pacifist logic was formed primarily in the context of very personal, face-to-face relationships and in the context of war between defined nation states. There is now a new dynamic in play, as an organized and perhaps quite entrenched cadre of committed terrorists representing no defined nation state and presenting no face-to-face presence among us moves to destroy lives of countless hundreds and thousands of people with no tangibly stated goals or positions for negotiation.

Such a situation calls forth in each of us a deeply reactive desire, on our own behalf and that of our families, to be defended from and protected against such horrible killing. Pacifists pushed to assert no desire for such defense and protection have let their rhetoric get out in front of honest emotions, honest introspection, and honest reasoning. Acknowledging this deeply human desire for protection and defense is the foundational step in seeking common ground between pacifists and our fellow citizens.

Exploring the logic of responsible pacifist citizenship in this time of a touted war on terrorism, we should expect a broadly based agreement among reflective citizens, pacifists and nonpacifists alike, on at least the following:

A deep-seated desire for defense and protection need not and should not entail an emotionally driven blanket sanction for any and all action against this terrorist force. Even in the face of this terrible evil we have, each one of us as citizens, an obligation to keep some kind of moral vision on our mental horizons beyond that of just vengeful striking out in all directions.

First, only actions of defense and protection in which the direct and indirect damage is outweighed by the realistic prospect of further terrorist actions should even be considered. In other words, defense against terrorism cannot now be used to sanction actions long deemed to be in the strategic and economic interests of the national security state but not undertaken because before September 11 we lacked a moral rationalization for doing so.

Second, of those actions of defense and protection that pass the first litmus test, only those most likely actually to reduce the risk of future terrorist actions should be implemented.

Finally, of those actions implemented, utmost care should be taken in the acts of implementation to preserve and respect those values and ethics our society holds in highest regard. Specifically, extreme care must be taken not to spread this conflict by framing it as one between religions or cultures. At present, the September 11 terrorists have been condemned by all but the most isolated, sliver segments of all societies and religions. However, that sliver will likely grow if the dominant framing of this conflict sets cultures or religions against one another.

Likewise, if the United States pursues actions in which large collateral damage is regularly inflicted predominantly on members of one particular culture or religion (for example, destroying whole villages of people of one particular religion or culture to "get" the small handful of terrorists that may or may not be hiding there) this will only increase the already-existing tendency to frame the conflict in cultural and religious terms.

Such willy nilly actions must be resisted most strongly at the policy-setting level. But on all levels, chest-thumping militaristic rhetoric in general is bound to be counterproductive in this situation. Such rhetoric, by its nature, demands an identified category of "enemy" for its emotional force to work. When that cannot be identified by naming a nation state (as it cannot in this case) the emotional force of the rhetoric moves inevitably in the direction of naming some other category—and cultural or religious categories are then often pressed into service.

In light of the above criteria, it appears likely that the most effective actions of real defense and protection will be covert strikes by special forces—tracking, pursuing, and assassinating individual people, actions carried out with little publicity or public knowledge at all. Whether or not I, as a pacifist citizen, like or agree with this has little bearing on the fact that it will be and is already being done.

Here, then, the responsibility of all American citizens, pacifist and non-pacifist alike, is to ponder how we can ensure that such deadly force, unleashed for a specific purpose more or less outside the normal boundaries of democratic control, does not reach beyond that purpose, and that the force is dissolved once its purpose is achieved. One need not be a pacifist to recognize how much of our current predicament stems directly from the fact that we trained, armed, and unleashed certain forces for specific purposes that then, rather than dissolve, took on their own dynamics and turned to bite us. A formed deadly power force, like chest-thumping rhetoric, has a strong tendency to function by its own dynamics that may not conform to the original intentions of those who brought it into being.

Furthermore, there is ample historical and empirical evidence that human beings are prone to engage in escalating spirals of threat and violence from which, once the escalating spiral is in motion, they find it difficult, almost impossible, to disengage. There is an identifiable dynamic in this escalating spiral of violence that traps the participants in a vicious cycle of action and reaction driven not by measured assessment of the real situation but by unconscious emotional reaction to the perception of the enemy as an embodiment of evil.

A measured assessment of the real situation may prompt nations to erect systems of physical defense. Yet any measured assessment of real potential threat must also contain within it rational limits to the level of violence a society is willing to employ. It is exactly this barrier of rational limits that quickly erodes as the spiral of violence escalates. As the enemy is increasingly perceived not as fellow human beings but as the symbolic embodiment of evil (thus subordinating the conscious and reasoning aspect of the human thought process to the residual unconscious aspect of human thought) the lines of rational control are extremely vulnerable to incremental violation.

Recognition that human beings are by nature selfish, greedy, and power hungry is often set forth by the ethical realists as the trump card against pacifist logic. Yet the major flaw in this realist perspective is the assumption that, because our cause is "just," we can somehow train and unleash human beings for deadly service outside boundaries of normal democratic control without these humans themselves also being affected by selfishness, greed, and hunger for power. Claiming to be "realistic" about human nature (in contrast to the "naïve" pacifist) the militarists almost invariably seem to think that somehow "we" are able to stand outside of that nature. Our enemies are selfish, greedy, and power hungry, hence must be resisted with deadly force. Yet it is rarely taken seriously that our wielders of deadly force are corrupted by or subject to becoming corrupted by these same tendencies of human nature.

Seen in this light, for citizens to unite in lockstep, as we are being called to do, granting the government and its military *carte blanche* for whatever is deemed necessary, is exactly the wrong way to go, not primarily because violent means are being used (that will happen whether we like it or not) but because it is naïve and unrealistic about the dynamics of power in this world, thus making it more likely that this force will be used outside the boundaries of original intention and will not dissolve once its original purposes are achieved.

There is little question that this deadly force, silent and outside of the boundaries of democratic control, will be unleashed. That is a likelihood nearly as undeniable as the wind and the rain, and not something any citizen, pacifist or otherwise, can alter. The burning issue before us as citizens is how we can use the political procedures available to us to best ensure that this force will place on itself some self-imposed controls for which there is no existing democratic enforcement mechanism, and that once its purpose is accomplished, this force will dissolve and the normal channels of democratic control on our military will be reestablished.

We do not control the immediate military action of our government. It will do what it will do apart from our desires or wishes and it is not up to us to make sure history will come out right on this. I recently heard Mennonite theologian Gayle Gerber Koontz speak on this issue with considerable wisdom.[1] She noted that when for years on end, despite urgings to the contrary, our nation has pursued policies in which corporate economic and national security self-interest have trumped the cries for considerations of justice, pacifists cannot then be expected to have some magical nonviolent solutions to situations of cyclical reactive violence when these occur.

To a large extent, then, the situation will have to play itself out according to the logic in force, after which there may again be opportunities to speak for more broadly based policies of justice and nonviolence. Although my focus here is on militarism, this brings home the point that the role of peacemaking is broader than only abjuring the use of violence in specific situations. Recognition by the wider society of the integrity and worth of the pacifist element among the citizenry is tied intimately to these broader commitments of activist peacemaking.

We pacifists also need to acknowledge that we do benefit significantly by the defense and protection against further terrorist attack likely to result from a concerted governmental and military effort to locate, identify, and destroy terrorist activists. Because we do benefit from such policies, it is our responsibility, as citizens with a vision of the good that goes far beyond that which can be accomplished by military force, to join with other significant sectors of our fellow citizens in offering constant, consistent, vocal, public, peaceful, loyal opposition to this government policy; to resist all *carte blanche* allocations of resources; and to scrutinize even more strongly than usual the areas of government and military action and policy in those places where channels of democratic control do continue to exist.

The natural human desire for defense and protection is strong; there will always be plenty of people offering the government its unquestioning support. If we simply join them in this, waving yet one more flag in the patriotic parade, we are but salt without savor, not taking seriously our role as citizens with a realistic understanding of human nature.

The commonplace standard is that the morality of an action can be tested by the question of what would result if "Everyone did it?" Hence, antimilitarist advocacy is viewed by many as obviously wrong in this case, since "What would happen if everyone thought that way and no one was willing to resist terrorism by force?" But this facile dismissal of pacifist social logic is both flawed and democratically unsophisticated.

In the first place, there is no danger of not having enough people to offer the government and its military their unswerving support. To assume otherwise is simply naïve about human beings and their nature. That human beings in overwhelming numbers will exchange freedom for security is surely one of the most well-established particulars of what we know about our species.

Second, this type of moral reasoning, while useful for navigating many moral dilemmas, is also unsophisticated about the politics required to maintain an ideologically diverse and pluralistic democratic society. Sophisticated political reasoning in a democratic context begins with the very opposite assumption than that all people will agree with or follow one given path or perspective. It is contrary to the very nature of democratic pluralism to base a policy on an assumed unity of paths or perspectives.

Furthermore, our factional diversity should not to be viewed as a temporary inconvenience or handicap to be overcome. Our diversity should be encouraged, even celebrated as an end in itself—it is our very foretaste of God's kingdom of freedom, to wax poetic for a moment. It is this very diversity that lends whatever moral integrity is left in the American claim that in our international relations we offer the peoples of this world a vision transcending the naked self-interests of the corporate national security state.

Therefore, we should not be reticent or embarrassed about jettisoning this commonplace type pf moral reasoning as our guide in this case. There is no danger that there will be a shortage of fellow citizens willing to offer their support for militaristic government policies. There is plenty of danger, however, of not having enough people to demonstrate to government the kind of stolid resistance required to dissuade those who execute such militaristic policies from the natural temptation of eventually using the power made available by the unleashing of deadly force outside of democratic controls, to pursue their own selfish, greedy, or power-hungry ends.

Those citizens, both pacifist and others, who have a realistic understanding of human nature know there is a compelling need to provide for our fellow humans in executive positions a counterbalance to the inherent tendencies of human nature to co-opt the use of power for selfish ends. We must place whatever weight our role as citizens has behind actions providing this counterbalance. Such actions need not be based on misguided and obsolete expectations of moral purity, nor is the integrity of these actions dependent on disavowing the reality of the protection and security that all citizens, including pacifist ones, gain from militaristic governmental policies.

In summary, what September 11 has shown is that pacifist citizens are not and cannot be isolated from terrible acts of overt violence. Thus we are exposed along with our fellow citizens to the raw emotions of fear, dread, and panic that being so targeted induces. The naked power of such emotions is a new experience for many of us, as well as is the corresponding power of the desire for protection and defense this situation has called forth in our breasts.

In our more rational minds, however, we have known that several centuries of insulation from acts of war on our home turf has been little more than an accident of geography, and that the shoe has been poised to drop for some time already. Much as we need to be ready and willing to acknowledge our desire for defense and protection against the terror we have tasted, as loyal, pacifist citizens of the Unites States and of the world, our place is is with those who resist the military policies and military consumption that are likley on the horizon for our nation. Our role includes joining those who criticize and debunk the chest-thumping militaristic rhetoric to which we will be increasingly exposed, especially when that rhetoric veers into claims of divine sanction for our violence.

NOTES

INTRODUCTION

1. Liechty (1990). The text reflects mainly stylistic changes, except chapters seven and eight, which are substantively revised or completely new. Substantive revisions in other chapters will appear in short excurses following some chapters, and in the endnotes.

2. Borg (1995). Related here is the work of the Jesus Seminar, which has received considerable attention in the popular press. Critics of the Jesus Seminar are convinced that this can only undermine public confidence in Christian truth and is ultimately destructive to Christian faith. Yet I have never met anyone nor read anything written by a person who was a confident believer in Christian truth whose faith and confidence were then destroyed by acquaintance with the Jesus Seminar material. I have, however, met many people who have been deeply touched by the writings on Jesus that have emerged from Jesus Seminar participants and who report that their Christian faith has been genuinely and sincerely revitalized by this material. Cf. Crossan and Watts (1999.)

3. Liechty (2000).

4. I have found myself repeatedly returning to Reinhold Niebuhr's anthropological writings for further reflection, especially Niebuhr (1941). MacQuarrie (1963) is the source from which I first saw Niebuhr's work characterized as *postliberal*.

5. Lindbeck (1984).

6. Kaufman (1985b). I should note that my view in general has been strongly influenced by the work of Gordon D. Kaufman (1972, 1975, 1981, 1985a, 1993, and 1995).

7. Among Mennonite sources, Gordon D. Kaufman's work should be especially noted for its generously spirited encounter with Buddhist sources. Also noteworthy in this regard, growing out of experience living in India, is the dialogical reflection of Dorothy Yoder Nyce (2000).

8. More recent works by Mennonites seem to lean toward a mediating position in which it is stressed that Christian faith is *unique* (different from other religions) and *relevant* (of value) to all people of all faiths, but that consciously downplay the conservative and neo-orthodox claims

that Christian truth is *normative* for all people and that the Christian religion is *superior* to other religions. Cf. here as examples, Shenk (1995 and 1997) and the essays in Stutzman and Shenk (1999). For the most part, I see this view as quite compatible with what I am advocating in this book. I would point especially here to the chapter by Susan Bieseker-Mast (1999). Bieseker-Mast speaks of an *aporetic* witness to Christian faith. *Aporea* is a philosophical term meaning an attitude of suspended judgment. Bieseker-Mast advocates that as much as we are ready to speak of Christian truth as we know it, in relation to other faith traditions we must also be just as ready to admit our lack of knowledge in an attitude of suspended judgment and be ready to be instructed by other faith traditions. My view is basically the same, but with the recognition that, if for nothing than more simple balance, it is high time for Western Christians primarily to assume the attitude of listening and learning.

9. Carroll (2001).

10. One of the most encouraging endeavors I have seen in this regard, both in terms of its process and results, was the consultation to further Christian and Jewish understanding held in June 1984, sponsored by the Shofar Committee under the auspices of The Eastern Mennonite Board of Missions and Charities of Salunga, PA. During a two-day joint meeting between the Shofar Committee, Eastern Board staff and invited Mennonite participants, representing Mennonite views, and two rabbis and two Jewish college professors, representing Jewish views, dialogue of obvious depth occurred, focused on issues of salvation, Messiah, land and community. The resulting document (EMBMC 1985) is, in my view, one of the very best available in the sizable literature of Jewish and Christian consultations. Unfortunately, it doesn't appear that there was any follow up at all from this promising beginning, the resulting document is no longer available, and in my inquiries to the offices of Eastern Board for more information concerning this consultation (its background, who participated, etc.) I was informed that no such information was kept in the historical record.

11. Brown (1961).

12. Both J. Denny Weaver (2000) and Ted Grimsrud (2000) are recent Mennonite theologians who have been quite explicit about their desire to construct a consistently pacifistic view in their theological writings. While I am offering here only reflections, and not theology proper, I would be pleased if what I have to offer were considered in conjunction with the recent, more explicitly theological works of these two writers.

13. Liechty (1986 and 1999b).

14. My work on a Christian theology of anarchy was done as a 1978 MA thesis. Both Vernard Eller (1987) and Jacques Ellul (1991), on whose earlier writings I drew heavily for my thesis, also published works of similar conclusions a decade later. I was pleased by this confirmation that I had correctly read the implications of their earlier work.

15. Liechty (1995, 1998a, 1998b, 1999a).

16. Liechty (2003).

17. Becker (1968, 1971, 1973 and 1975).

18. This research is called *Terror Management Theory* in the specialized literature and includes many dozens of published studies. Summary statements of this ongoing research and its results can be found in Solomon, *et al.* (1991), Greenberg, *et al.* (1997) and Solomon, et al. (1998).

19. Sam Keen (1974) interviewed Becker in the hospital a few days before Becker died.

CHAPTER ONE

1. That religious reflection must proceed from an unavoidable awareness of the human situation in which our species has assumed the ability to extinguish itself has been the theme of two different but related bodies of writing for at least a generation already. These two bodies of writing are those dealing with post-Holocaust theology, focusing on the history of antisemitism and genocide against the Jewish people of Europe, and post-Hiroshima theology, focusing on the human situation in the context of weapons of mass destruction. Examples of post-Holocaust approaches are found in Fleischner, ed. (1977), Cargas, ed. (1981), and especially Katz (1983). Examples of post-Hiroshima approaches are Kaufman (1985a), Chernus (1983), Auckerman (1989), Grannis, Laffin and Schade (1981), and Weigert (1988). There is now an important and growing literature focused on the reality of environmental destruction and a *posthuman future* as a result of genomic tampering. For examples of this approach, see Committee (1998), Nelson (1994), Rantala and Milgram (1999), and Kass (2001).

2. We have seen this misuse of scientific theory and evidence recently in the writings of prominent sociobiologists and evolutionary psychologists. There the assumption is that once 'science' has spoken concerning any aspect of human existence, it is an affront that other perspectives would offer any conflicting views. Examples here include Dawkins (1998), Wright (1995) and various essays in Barkow, et al. (1995).

3. Voegelin (1966).

4. Most values and mores, however, become simply neutral in changing historical circumstances, creating that large pool of rich, human behavioral diversity that adds so much color to our life. Multicultural experience and education at its best is aimed at helping us sort out in particular circumstances the positive, the negative and the neutral in human diversity, and to enhance the positive, criticize and alter the negative, and to enjoy the richness of the neutral.

5. In the first place the work of the religious reflection should be iconoclastic—*unlearning* much of the cultural images of power and authority picked up in the socialization process. However, we also eventually move beyond mere iconoclasm and, while retaining a strong sense of critical skepticism, begin to construct new understandings and formulations of responsible religious thought.

6. My use of the term *located* in this regard is not meant to ignore or even take a particular position in the rapidly changing range of possible

views concerning the relationship between mind and brain. It does seem logical, however, that there could be brain without mind, but not the reverse. Mind is what brain does. For purpose here, I don't need to solve that conundrum to make my point.

7. Here I am explicitly connecting my view of the human soul and spirit to the view called *nonreductive physicalism*, which is being explicated especially by Nancey Murphy and her colleagues at Fuller Theological Seminary. See Brown, Murphy and Maloney (1998).

8. Becker (1973). For a penetrating extension of Becker's point of view from a specifically theological perspective, see Westphal (1987). For philosophically informed approaches, see Fischer (1993), Kauffman (1995) and Fingarette (1996).

9. Nietzsche (1966).

10. Vahanian (1966).

11. This is one of the central and enduring phenomenological observations in Sartre (1968). See more recently Chancer (1992) and Brandt (1986).

12. Cf. here, for example, Keen (1986); Becker (1975); Barnett (1977); Chernus (1983). Instructive also is Duster (1971).

13. We do not have in America any developed tradition for the study of heretics. In the American context, heresy (literally, choosing for oneself in matters of religious belief) is part of our religious heritage and our sense of human rights. However, in Europe, the study of *Ketzergeschichte* has a long history. While for centuries the evaluation of heretics was negative, there is also positive evaluation even among the most respected scholars. Cf., for example, Nigg (1949) and the numerous essays collected in Schultz, ed. (1968)

14. Lakoff and Johnson (1999).

15. A few of examples of such metaphors are affection is warm; big is important; happy is up; bad is foul-smelling; knowing is seeing. Examples of such oppositions are up/down; inner/outer; over/under.

16. Cf. Brown, Murphy and Maloney (1998).

CHAPTER TWO

1. Rougemont (1941)

2. Many names could be mentioned in this context. Most important for my reflections are Wilhelm Reich (1971), Otto Rank (1971), Norman O. Brown (1959), Erich Fromm (1973), Robert J. Lifton (1979, 1990), Ervin Straub (1989), Paul Ricoeur (1969), Ernest Becker (1968, 1975), and Merold Westphal (1984).

3. Becker (1975), p. 96.

4. Paul Carus (1969) is very informative. See also Jeffrey B. Russell (1977, 1981, 1984, 1988).

5. This parallels closely the use of this concept, presented in a literary context, in Girard, (1977, 1986). For application of this theory of scapegoating to social criticism, see Bailie (1995). See also the more theologically astute working of Girard's ideas in Schwager (1987) and especially Williams (1991).

6. That there is no shortage of religious leaders, both liberal and conservative, ready and willing to give God's blessing to America during international conflict is confirmed in the study of Abrams (1969).

7. Becker (1975), pp. 150 and 153.

8. Keen (1986).

9. I have been taking every opportunity for the past few years to draw close attention to the work of former military psychologist Lt. Col. (ret.) David Grossman (1997). Grossman spent his military career perfecting methods in basic training for overcoming young soldiers' aversions to brutality and killing. Eventually, Grossman was disturbed that, as might be expected, many soldiers who had been through this kind of training and acted it out on the battlefield were returning to civilian life and finding it very difficult to adjust. But even more disturbing, Grossman started to notice very clear parallels between the techniques which had been developed in the military to overcome reluctance to kill (such as desensitization to violence, classical and operant conditioning, role modeling, dehumanization of the targets, etc.) and that which young people are exposed to on a daily basis on TV, films, video games, certain types of music, and other areas of that which Grossman calls the "violence-as-entertainment" media. Drawing on further research as well as on cultural sources, Grossman powerfully suggests that while it may not be possible to take any one of these media in isolation and say, "This causes increased violence in our youth and in society," taken together, a very clear Gestalt begins to emerge, forming what Grossman calls a "virus of violence," infecting a society suffering from a syndrome of acquired violence immunity deficiency. See also (parents!) Grossman and DeGaetano (1999).

10. This recognition that any God can be either an idol or a source of critical strength in moving away from idols (with comfortable Gods more likely of the former type) is a major point of agreement between the theoretical works of Ernest Becker and René Girard. Becker's work is much more accessible to social scientists, while Girard's work appears to be more accessible to literary scholars. I am pleased that Mennonite theologians (Swartley 2000) have given sustained attention to Girard's ideas, particularly as these relate to the problem of violence and peacemaking. Equal attention to Becker's work could provide the connection to the social sciences that is currently lacking in this endeavor.

11. One of the most valuable Mennonite contributions here is Friesen (1986).

12. I realize that I am stating this ethical commitment quite cautiously—perhaps more cautiously than is warranted—probably a reflection of my social science training. I want to connect my reflections here to very positively presented statements of the same ethical commitment, however, that make clear the dialectic of action and critical reflection. A very deep yet accessibly written recent example, which stresses the theological and biblical background, is Ted Grimsrud (2000).

13. Wink (1984, 1986, 1992, and 1998).

14. Papers of this conference are intended for publication at some point. For the time being, my paper, in only slightly altered form, can be

found at website of the Ernest Becker Foundation, http://www.ernest-becker.org.

CHAPTER THREE

1. The thesis that our concept of God arises in the context of our search for meaning and purpose in life (Tillich's category of "Ultimate Concern") is thoroughly supported in the psychology of religion. I have been most influenced in my particular view by Viktor Frankl and the "Third Vienna School" of logotherapy. Among the many works of Frankl, most notable in this context is Frankl (1977). Cf. also Bulka (1979). More general views supporting the same contention are found in Hocking (1957); Fowler (1981); and Becker (1971, 1973). More recent psychological investigations have focused on the positive power of God concepts in building coping skills and other benefits.

2. Although the theory of natural selection has taken a large bite out of the conviction inspired by the argument from design for the existence of God in classical philosophy of religion, the intricacy of the natural world still remains very much a source of religious awe. Although in my view it thoroughly confuses spiritual intuition with scientific theory, it is worth noting the recent resurgence of apologetic interest in "intelligent design theory." Cf. Demski and Behe (1999).

3. Eco-philosopher David Abram (1996) masterfully explored the shifts in consciousness that take place in the transition from preliterate to modern cultures, a process that effectively cuts people off from a meaningful sense of connection to the more-than-human world. Cf. also Liechty (2000).

4. In the past decade alone, we have seen it become commonly accepted, both in practice and in attitude, that *medical care* and treatment should be dictated by the concern of large managed care companies to return profits to investors, as well as the beginnings of investor-based for-profit ventures into *higher education* and *child rearing*. We hardly seem to remember that just a few years ago we considered these areas of life somehow sacrosanct and separate from crude market-driven decision making.

5. Bellah, et al. (1985, 1987, 1991). I am particularly encouraged by the rise of explicitly communitarian ideas in social theory. Cf. Etzioni (1998).

6. Fischer and Lasch, (1988); Lasch (1989); Coontz (1992).

7. Gramsci (1957).

8. It will be clear to the reader by now that I generally follow a post-critical approach to this question. I do not think that evidence for the existence of God is overwhelmingly compelling, especially in light of the real problem of evil. Not just human evil and the innocent suffering it brings casts doubt on the existence of God, but the realization that we find ourselves in an environment in which, even in the best of circumstances, life sustains itself only by ripping at, gnawing at, destroying, ingesting, digesting and expelling other life. Much as I share in that grateful sense that this world is a good place in which to live, a gift of the Cre-

ator, I speak as one relatively high up in the food chain. For most of the world's creatures, if they were conscious of their real situation, existence in this world would be little more than a constant nightmare, an eternal torture chamber. I think we humans may have more of this sense in our collective memory than we would like to admit. Barbara Ehrenreich (1997) makes the very plausible suggestion that for all but the most recent centuries of our species history (when brain development finally allowed us to grasp the concept of external weapons) we were among the prey species and not the predators. (Ehrenreich's connection of this transition from prey to predator species with our continuing fascination with weapons technology dovetails neatly with our view that such weapons represent for us an extremely strong immortality fetish.)

On the other hand, I do not think that to believe in God's existence one must make blind, implausible leaps over logical chasms, nor place one's intellect in a safe deposit box. Traditional theology has long held that belief is itself a gift, and I am pleased to leave it at that. It is a gift I share sometimes, and not at other times. All the same, I reject the commonplace assumption that the division between belief and unbelief is the most essential dividing point, even for religious reflection. I know without question that believer and unbeliever can coexist peacefully, mutually respectfully, even creatively, each contributing to the wider human project of seeking meaning, wholeness and purpose in life—for they do so inside of me.

9. Among modern theologians, it is Gordon D. Kaufman who has pursued most consistently the theme of theology as a positive, constructive task. See especially Kaufman (1975 and 1981). Crucial here also are McFague (1987); McCoy (1980); Pohier (1977, 1985); Kung and Tracy (1984, 1986). Of course the idea of reality construction was always implicit in the sociology of knowledge. Cf., for example, Holzner (1967). It was only a matter of applying the insights of reality construction to theology for it to become explicit that theology is a constructive rather than descriptive effort. It is most fitting that sociologist of religion Peter L. Berger (1979), who with Thomas Luckmann introduced many of us to the concept of reality as socially constructed, made just this explicit application.

10. Gazzaniga (1994).

CHAPTER FOUR

1. One of the most expanding and joyful experiences of learning I have had in associating closely with two synagogues is the slowly dawning realization that my Christian background had given me a totally skewed concept of Torah. Even having gained two graduate degrees in theology, I still basically understood Torah as religious Law. Typically, in this conception, Torah implicitly contrasts negatively to such concepts as divine grace, spiritual freedom and unconditional love. I have come to understand that this is absolutely contrary to a Jewish conception of Torah. Torah encompasses the divine execution and integrally moral character

of the universe itself, its discovered and yet to be discovered physical and scientific principles; the principles by which human society may operate to the maximum benefit of each member; and the basic moral disposition of each individual that is most pleasing to the divine. Torah is inextricable from, or even identical with, God's *hesed*, God's loving-kindness, pouring out to all of creation and to each individual. How different this is from some sort of oppressive, divinely imposed legal standard by which we are inevitably condemned and from which we must then appeal for escape, to have it, as a burden, lifted from us. How refreshing it has been to go back and read with new eyes the biblical and book of services passages in which Torah is present. "Open my heart to Your Torah, that I may know how to answer Your Call."

This misunderstanding of Torah is but one example of the truly spiritually impoverished state in which the 'triumph' of church over synagogue left Christians. The conflict between self-righteous legalism and gracious freedom is a very real conflict. But it is a conflict *within the Christian body itself*, not a conflict between divine Torah and divine Grace, and most certainly not a conflict between synagogue and church, or between Judaism and Christianity. Excising these destructive sinews of triumphant Christian anti-Judaism from Christian ideology is not just an imperative of polite civility, as if by this we would be doing someone else a favor. It is an imperative for the spiritual health of the Christian body itself.

2. This theme comes through in no place so clearly as in the "Magnificat" of Mary, Luke 1:46ff. A significant systematic treatment of this passage is Walsh (1987). See also the essays collected in Schrottroff and Stegemann (1984).

3. Cf. Gottwald (1979).

4. Gottwald (1986).

5. Gottwald (1983); Lind (1990).

6. Cf. Crusemann (1978). Somewhat less to the point, but much better known, is Walzer (1985).

7. Monotheism can function as a religious support system for absolute monarchy and tyranny—one God, one king, one Fuehrer. It is not monotheism itself, but rather a system in which loyalty to the ruler is ordered through loyalty to God, instead of loyalty to God being ordered through loyalty to the king, that monotheism stands as a relativizing factor to the power of would-be tyrants. For a feminist perspective on this issue, see Falk (1989).

8. Hengel (1974).

9. This sense of living on through one's children as symbolic immortality is given very sensitive and positive treatment by Robert Jay Lifton (1979). Bregman (1984) offers an insightful comparison of the views of Ernest Becker and Robert Jay Lifton on the psychology of symbolizing immortality.

10. See here especially Yoder (1972); Hengel (1977); Horsley (1993).

11. Cf. Yoder (1972), pp. 26ff.; Hengel (1973).

12.The importance of this tradition is most thoroughly discussed in Lind (1980), pp. 91ff.

13.Cf. here Durrant (1973).

14.One recent historian has presented strong evidence that the first century Jewish Platonic philosopher Philo of Alexandria formulated the notion of a 'second god' in heaven whose duty it was to carry out divine action on earth in an attempt to defend the immutability (unchanging nature) of the higher God. This was picked up from Philo by Justin and there entered into the stream of Christian thought that eventually emerged in the trinitarian dogma. (Cf. Segal 1999)

15.Friesen (2000).

16.Ibid. 89.

17.Nelson-Pallmeyer (2001). Nelson-Pallmeyer's work is the most recent to make this argument, and he does so with unusual thoroughness; however, the basic points have been around for decades and so should be examined in any pacifist-intentioned treatment of the trinitarian dogma. Also noteworthy in this regard is the claim of Clarence Bauman (1993, p. 136) that we too quickly exchange the *way* of the cross for a *theology* of the cross, which is a natural move once we have established a creedal, trinitarian view that jumps right over the whole of Jesus' actual life.

18.Weaver (2000).

19.Finger (1989), 445n and 451n.

20.Reimer (2001), 392-405. Unfortunately, this veil of silence concerning nontrinitarian views within the Mennonite tradition is not limited to Mennonite thought of past centuries. Mitchell Brown, a theologically trained Mennonite pastor of Jewish background, published a very insightful article suggesting an authentic nontrinitarian approach to Mennonite theology. (Brown 1987) Brown's work thus far has been greeted with all but complete silence from the Mennonite theologians.

CHAPTER FIVE

1. Marxsen (N.D.).

2. Cf. Sheehan (1986), pp. 175ff.; Schillebeeckx (1979), 320ff.; Bornkamm (1971), pp. 203-9.

3. Perrin (1963, 1967) and Schillebeeckx (1979), pp. 105ff. Very interesting in this regard are books being written by Jewish New Testament scholars, since these scholars are less likely than their Christian counterparts to interpret the texts recording the preaching of Jesus in traditionally Christian ways. See as one example Lapide (1980). Also of interest here is Neusner (1993).

4. Perrin (1968). Cf. also the essays collected in Braaten and Harrisville, eds. (1964); Sheehan (1986), pp. 183ff.

5. This view has been present in New Testament scholarship since the late nineteenth century. Recently it has been given theological treatment in Driver (1981). Cf. also Segundo (1988).

6. Compare this view to Bousset (1970). Although neither uses the ter-

minology of a tactic of survival, and they discuss the issue specifically in relation to early Christian refusal to serve in the military, the view that the exclamation *"Kyrios Christos"* functioned in this capacity is strongly present in Harnack (1981) and in Hornus (1980). Cf. also Bainton (1960), pp. 66ff., and Childress (1986), pp. 117ff.

7. Berger (1974).

8. That we are responsible for what we teach about Christ (rather than simply passers-on of received tradition) was made most clear to me by Tom Driver's chapter "Method for an Ethical Christology," in Driver (1981), pp. 12ff.

9. My first formulation of what follows was presented in the context of Christian dialogue with Marxist perspectives on salvation. Cf. Liechty (1984)

10. Liechty (1996). It is in this context again that we touch base with the current theme of the "priority of the poor" which is central to the so-called theology of liberation. A good example here is Boff (1988). This by no means should imply that the task of the theologian is simply to articulate in academic language and present as 'truth' whatever religious ideas are present among the least powerful segments of the society. There are many nasty and brutish religious notions there as well, no matter how much we are tempted to idealize the wisdom of the oppressed. Cf. Lanternari (1965). Numerous other works could be cited for this point. While there is no attempt here to idealize the wisdom of the oppressed, it is my intention to call religious seekers to search out among the least powerful segments of society that 'principled atheism' toward notions of God most current in the society and to allow this principled atheism to function in a critical capacity in theological construction.

11. Schillebeeckx (1979), pp. 379ff.; Driver (1981), pp. 32ff.; Sheehan, (1986), pp. 206ff.

12. Schubert Ogden has been taken to task for his formulations of a theology of liberation. The complaint against him is that he must, finally, make a clear, categorical separation between 'redemption' and 'emancipation' in his theology. Redemption is viewed as metaphysical redemption from 'sin and death,' while emancipation is viewed as liberation from concrete, present situations of oppression. Cf. Min (1989). The view I am supporting here, that we construct our teachings of being redeemed on an ethical stance toward the world, is, I think, immune to this criticism. I do think, however, that Ogden is correct in insisting that some sort of 'metaphysical' perspective on the human situation is a much needed corrective in the struggle for emancipation, where the focus is too easily collapsed completely into a political or economic vision of emancipation. I find Jesus' relationship with the Zealot movement in his time is instructive, but, like most of Jesus' teaching and example, it is not unambiguous or leading to only one possible conclusion.

13. The consummate statement of this view remains Cullmann (1950).

14. A criticism of sacramental theology from this perspective is offered in Yoder (1984).

15. The classic work is the monumental six-volume commentary, Billerbeck and Strack (1922-1963).

16. According to a poster hanging in the hallway of the Vienna Meeting of the Religious Society of Friends, the following is attributed to George Fox: "Christ said this, the apostles said that—but what canst thou say?" This captures exactly the message I am trying to express here.

17. The penetrating question posed by Driver (1981). Also helpful here is Knitter (1985).

18. Nyce (2000).

CHAPTER SIX

1. This illustrates the importance of having a firm grounding in at least one of the foundational cultural literary traditions, such as the Bible, Shakespeare, the Greco-Roman literature. It fosters an ongoing and mutually interpretive dialogue between individual and shared group experience. Such literature draws the community of readers, interpreters and memorizers into a broad framework of narrative meaning that creates a web of personal and communal meaning and sense-making for living in this world.

2. Therefore, for example, in relating to the English reader the richness of the world of the French peasant, author John Berger (1979) felt the need to include a lengthy foreword and afterword, drawing the reader into the thought structure of the peasants. This is not because the English reader would not understand the *words* of the stories—all were related in English. Berger knew, rather, that without at least some limited attempt to bring to the English reader some window of understanding into the cultural context of the French peasants, an understanding of the stories themselves was impossible.

3. Words are symbols. On the human being as a symbolic animal, see Becker (1971), pp 13ff. Deacon (1997) extends this analysis to demonstrate the key role that language development played in the evolution of the human brain. Some philosophers, such as Susanne Langer (1957), have claimed that there are nondiscursive languages with grammar structure but no semantic structure. Therefore, for example, people sharing no common language can communicate through music. This is probably true, but also assumes some common grounding in cultural experience. That music is meant to 'communicate' at all, and that one listens to it for that purpose, is something that must be learned.

4. Rapoport (1954).

5. By spiritual life, I mean inner experience of the world on which one can reflect, but which is not possible fully to articulate in language. Attempts to articulate such inner experience are always and only partial and approximations (cf. Romans 8:26).

6. When I characterize a moral and ethical stance in the world as pacifistic, it must be understood that I am speaking in the broadest sense— that of a pacific (peaceful) approach toward life and others that does not assume that violent conflict is inevitable (and therefore does not prepare

in advance for such conflict by, for example, carrying weapons.) It is an approach to life that strives to seek reconciliation when conflict does occur, not punishment or revenge. It is much more than an abjuring of participation in armed conflict. It is not assumed that committed pacifists will agree with each other in lock step on every application of these principles to specific situations such as medical, economic and social issues. Furthermore, commitment to a pacifistic ethic is no grounds for moral self-righteousness—as if all who disagree are immoral. It is unfortunate that because pacifists often express themselves in moralistic tones, they are often perceived this way. However, I do unapologetically assume a close relationship between a progressively pacifistic stand in the world and genuinely Christian morality and ethics.

The Mennonite tradition in which I was raised strongly emphasized the theme of *Nachfolge Christi* (following the way of Jesus) as the heart of the Christian life. Perhaps this is naïve or simplistic, but it is difficult for me to conceive of the Christian life in any terms that diametrically oppose the model of following the way of Jesus. Following the way of Jesus, looking to Jesus as a model, integrating the 'Jesus factor' into one's life—if there is no interest in that, even if it be only in terms of an integration dialectically conceived with some other norm, I cannot see the point in calling oneself Christian at all. As I look at the portrait of the life of Jesus as it has been handed down to us by tradition, it seems inevitable to me that as one brings the 'Jesus factor' into one's life, one will be moving toward an increasingly pacifistic ethic.

7. I worked for some years as a group specialist in an inpatient mental hospital. During that time I consulted on cases in which strong religious ideations were present. There I saw first hand how closely our most emotionally intensive understandings of God are affected by early childhood experiences of parents and adult caregivers. Cf. Rizzuto (2001) and Fischer (2001). Pacifistic people tend to be those who have established at a very young age a sense of the *basic trustworthiness* of reality. Those who do not have this instilled sense of the basic trustworthiness of reality find it much more difficult to accept the personal vulnerability of pacifistic commitment. This emerging understanding of how important such early experiences are in shaping the contours of later life places a historical imperative on pacifistic communities to eliminate emotional, physical and sexual abuse in the raising of their own children and to work cooperatively in whatever ways possible for the elimination of these evils in the larger society.

8. The fact that they state clearly their ethical stance in the world is a very strong reason why socially and politically conservative churches have experienced notable growth in the past 20 years. In times of social confusion, people are naturally drawn toward communal organizations that articulate a strong and consistent set of social expectations.

9. Cunliffe-Jones (1980) and McGiffert (1932) contain good summaries of these early Christian controversies. In addition, many collections and investigations exist on individual points of controversy in the early church. Our knowledge of early Christian pluralism has been greatly ex-

tended by recent studies of extra-biblical writings. However, it is present within the biblical materials themselves.

10. Munz (1964, 1977). In Munz's analysis, the symbol picture, or mythology, is a direct expression of spiritual experience. Metaphysics results from general observations about the symbol pictures taken as composites, i.e., metaphysical statements are a posteriori, synthetic statements and can be tested against the evidence of the symbol pictures.

11. Pagels (1979, 1988).

12. On Hans Denck, cf. Clarence Bauman (1990). On James Naylor, cf. Barbour and Roberts (1973).

CHAPTER SEVEN

1. By conservatives, I have in mind mainly the Protestant fundamentalists and Evangelicals simply because I know them the best. However, the same attitude of exclusivity is found among conservative Roman Catholics and other conservative traditionalists.

2. Cf. Anderson and Stransky (1975) pp. 239-48, for the full text of the concluding document of this important 1974 meeting in Lausanne, Switzerland.

3. The most clear statements are found in Barth (1956), pp. 280-361. A shortened version is found in Hick and Hebblethwaite (1980), pp. 32-51.

4. Cf. Rahner (1965ff.) vol. 12, pp. 161-78; and vol. 14, pp. 280-94.

5. Hans Kung (1976), pp. 89-118 and (1988), pp. 227ff.

6. Hick (1982; 1989; 1995).

7. Streng, et al (1973).

8. I am not here engaging the controversy as to whether or not scientific discovery, Marxism or other ideologies of political messianism, psychoanalysis, or secular humanism (whatever that is) should be interpreted as variant forms of *religion*. I am saying, however, that in seeking a broadly valid method for understanding the ways in which modern human beings pursue meaning and truth through religion, the validity of our method is strengthened by the observation that this same method easily encompasses also the major secular forms of philosophies and ideologies through which large numbers of modern human beings also pursue meaning and truth.

9. Making a similar point, Karen Armstrong (2000) cites a Talmudic interpretation in which the rabbis suggest that " . . . when God appeared to Moses on Mount Sinai, each of the Israelites standing around the foot of the mountain experienced God in an entirely different manner according to his or her personality. They also said that each one of the prophets had an entirely different experience of God because of his particular psyche" (p. 17).

10. Does the social environment create personality styles or do personality styles create the social environment? In another context, I would argue for the dialectic view in regard to this question of social psychology. For the purposes of this discussion, however, we can happily shelve that vexing question altogether.

11. Stability within a religion or religious subgroup may not be assured by reinforcing the dominant styles, but rather by encouraging the subdominant styles. For example, within American Judaism of the immediate post-War years, any mystical expressions were completely subdominant, even suppressed. One result of this was that especially young people who ached for that kind of spiritual connection were drawn elsewhere to find it—and one cannot help noticing, for example, the predominance of people of Jewish upbringing among the leadership of American Buddhism and other meditative movements that emerged during the late 1950s and 1960s. These "converts" sparked a renewed search within Judaism for a core spiritual Judaism (Gordis 1995) and this, in turn, awakened interest in the subdominant, mystical and meditative paths within Judaism. (Kamenetz 1994; Lerner 1994) Presently, American Jews seeking such a path are easily aware of the deep resources, such as Kabbalah and Hasidic ecstasy, that have been present all along within Judaism as a subdominant option. My sense is that such Jews today, as a result of this awareness, are much less likely to 'convert' to another religion and much more likely to explore these pathways of expression while remaining within Judaism (Boorstein 1997).

12. Thus we have Mennonites exploring contemplative and liturgical styles, monastic affiliation, mystical meditation and charismatic full-Gospel worship, while others acquainted to these styles are attracted to the Mennonite commitment to economic relief and active programs of social justice. Prominent Christian Evangelicals become Roman Catholic or Eastern Orthodox while Roman and Eastern Catholics become Christian Evangelicals.

13. Fowler (1981); Kegan (1983); Kohlberg (1981). Most recently, F. W. Schmidt (2000) has published a fine collection making this point (with accompanying videotape series also available.) But it is a point made long ago by J. B. Phillips (1952).

14. The little book by Richard J. Mouw (1994) is a good reminder of the value of specialist and lay understandings interacting with each other. I especially liked the approach Mouw characterized as a "hermeneutic of charity," in contrast to a hermeneutic of suspicion.

15. People who involve themselves in interreligious ideas are perhaps too eager to draw disparate sources into some kind of higher synthesis of religions. I do not take this to be the only goal, or even the best goal, of interreligious dialogue. It may even be evidence of an inability to accept genuine diversity and pluralism at a fundamental level. Rather than respond to the urge to establish a higher synthesis of religions, I would rather we first learn to live together in peace within religious diversity for at least a couple of generations. By then the natural mingling of traditions may perhaps eclipse concentrated efforts at finding a higher synthesis. More open dialogue is goal enough for now, a dialogue that does not seek synthesis but rather peaceful coexistence. Here I am strongly attracted to the idea of "unitive pluralism" found in Knitter (1985).

CHAPTER EIGHT

1. Martin (1978).
2. Newberg and D'Aquili (2001).
3. Loy (1996).
4. Rolheiser (1999).
5. St. John of the cross (1959).
6. Kierkegaard (1983).
7. The Jewish and Christian doctrine of the resurrection of the body is interesting in this regard since, in contrast to the more common idea of the immortality of the soul, it does appear to accept the mortal nature, while still holding out the possibility that death is not the end. Further explorations (Jewish and Christian respectively) of this contrast are found in Jacobs (1988) and Cullmann (1958). It should be noted that, despite the regular recitations of the creeds that include belief in the resurrection of the dead, the assumption that Christianity teaches the immortality of the soul continues apace.
8. Lifton (1979).
9. Ibid., pp. 8 and 13.
10. Liechty (1994).

APPENDIX 2

1. Gayle Gerber Koontz, speaking at a meeting of the Theological Forum, Normal Mennonite Church, Normal, Ill., December 9, 2001.

REFERENCES

Abram, D. (1996) *The Spell of the Sensuous: Perception and Language in a More-Than-Human World.* New York: Pantheon Books.

Abrams, R. H. (1969) *Preachers Present Arms.* Scottdale, Pa.: Herald Press.

Anderson, G. A. and Stransky, T. F. eds. (1975) *Mission Trends Number Two: Evangelization.* New York: Paulist Press.

Armstrong, K. (2000) The God of Imaginative Compassion. In F. W. Schmidt, ed. (pp. 15-31) *The Changing Face of God.* Harrisburg, Pa.: Morehouse Publishing.

Auckerman, D. (1989) *Darkening Valley: A Biblical Perspective on Nuclear War.* Scottdale, Pa.: Herald Press.

Bailie, G. (1995) *Violence Unveiled: Humanity at the Crossroads.* New York: Crossroad Publishing Company.

Bainton, R. H. (1960) *Christian Attitudes Toward War and Peace.* Nashville, Tenn.: Abingdon Press.

Barbour, H. and Roberts, A. O. (1973) *Early Quaker Writings, 1650-1700.* Grand Rapids, Mich.: Wm. B. Eerdmans.

Barkow, J. H., Cosmides, L., and Tooby, J. (1995) *The Adapted Mind: Evolutionary Psychology and the Generation of Culture.* New York: Oxford University Press.

Barnett, R. (1977) *The Giants.* Greenville, N.C.: S and S Publishing, Inc.

Barth, K. (1956) *Church Dogmatics, Vols. 1/2.* Edinburgh, UK: T. and T. Clark.

Bauman, C. (1990) *The Spiritual Legacy of Hans Denck: Interpretation and Translation of Key Texts.* Leiden, NL: E. J. Brill.

—— (1993) *On the Meaning of Life: An Anthology of Theological Reflection.* Nappanee, IN: Evangel Press.

Becker, E. (1968) *The Structure of Evil.* New York: George Braziller.

—— (1971) *The Birth and Death of Meaning: An Interdisciplinary Perspective on the Problem of Man.* New York: The Free Press.

—— (1973) *The Denial of Death.* New York: The Free Press.

—— (1975) *Escape from Evil.* New York: The Free Press.

Bellah, R. N., Madsen, R., Sullivan, W. M. and Tipton, S. M. (1985) *Habits of the Heart: Individualism and Commitment in American Life.* New York: Harper & Row.

Bellah, R. N., Madsen, R., Sullivan, W. M. and Tipton, S. M. (1987) *Individualism and Commitment in American Life.* New York: Harper & Row.

——— (1991) *The Good Society.* New York: Alfred Knopf.

Berger, J. (1979) *Pig Earth.* New York: Pantheon Books.

Berger, P. L. (1974) *Pyramids of Sacrifice: Political Ethics and Social Change.* New York: Doubleday.

——— (1979) *The Heretical Imperative: Contemporary Possibilities of Religious Affirmation.* New York: Doubleday.

Bieseker-Mast, S. (1999) The Aporetic Witness. In L. Stutzman and D. W. Shenk, eds. (pp. 130-147) *Practicing Truth: Confident Witness In Our Pluralistic World.* Scottdale, Pa.: Herald Press.

Billerbeck, P. (1922-1963) *Kommentar zum Neuen Testament aus Talmud und Midrasch.* Munich, Germany: C. H. Beck.

Boorstein, S. (1997) *That's Funny, You Don't Look Buddhist: On Being a Faithful Jew and a Passionate Buddhist.* San Francisco, CA: Harper Collins.

Borg, M. (1995) *Meeting Jesus Again for the First Time: The Historical Jesus and the Heart of Contemporary Faith.* San Francisco, CA: Harper San Francisco.

Bornkamm, G. (1971) The Risen Lord and the Earthly Jesus: Mt. 28:16-20. In J. M. Robinson, ed. (pp. 203-209) *The Future of Our Religious Past.* New York: Harper & Row.

Boff, L. (1988) *When Theology Listens to the Poor.* San Francisco, CA: Harper & Row.

Bousset, W. (1970) *Kyrios Christi.* Nashville, Tenn.: Abingdon Press.

Braaten, C. and Harrisville, R. eds. (1964) *The Historical Jesus and the Kerygmatic Christ.* Nashville, Tenn.: Abingdon Press.

Brandt, D. (1986) *Don't Stop Now, You're Killing Me: The Sadomasochism Game in Everyday Life.* New York: Poseidon Press.

Bregman, L. (1984) Three Psycho-Mythologies of Death: Becker, Hillman and Lifton. *Journal of the American Academy of Religion, 52 (3)* 461-79.

Brown, M. (1987) Jesus: Messiah Not God. *Conrad Grebel Review, 5,* 233-252.

Brown, N. O. (1959) *Life Against Death: The Psychoanalytical Meaning of History.* New York: Vintage Books.

Brown, R. M. (1961) *The Spirit of Protestantism.* New York: Oxford University Press.

Brown, W. S., Murphy, N. and Maloney, H.N. (1998). *Whatever Happened to the Soul? Scientific and Theological Portraits of Human Nature.* Minneapolis, Minn.: Fortress Press.

Bulka, R. P. (1979) *The Quest for Ultimate Meaning: Principles and Applications of Logotherapy.* New York: Philosophical Library.

Cargas, H.J. (1981) *When God and Man Failed.* New York: MacMillan.

Carroll, J. (2001) *Constantine's Sword: The Church and the Jews.* New York: Houghton Mifflin.

Carus, P. (1969) *The History of the Devil and the Idea of Evil From the Earliest Times to the Present Day.* New York: Bell Publ. Co.

Chancer, L. S. (1992) *Sadomasochism in Everyday Life: The Dynamics of Power and Powerlessness*. New Brunswick, N.J.: Rutgers University Press.

Chernus, I. (1983).The Symbolism of the Bomb. *Christian Century*, Oct. 12, 1983.

Childress, J. F. (1986) Moral Discourse About War in the Early Church. In P. Peachey, ed. (pp. 117-129) *Peace, Politics and the People of God*. Philadelphia: Fortress Press.

Committee on Medical Ethics, Episcopal Diocese of Washington, D.C. (1998). *Wrestling with the Future: Our Genes and Our Choices*. Harrisburg, Pa.: Morehouse Publishing.

Coontz, S. (1992) *The Way We Never Were: American Families and the Nostalgia Trap*. New York: Basic Books.

Crossan, J. D. and Watts, R. (1999) *Who Is Jesus? Answers to Your Questions About the Historical Jesus*. Louisville, Ky.: Westminster John Knox Press.

Crusemann, F. (1978) *Der Widerstand gegen das Konigtum: Die antikoniglichen Texte des Alten Testaments und der Kampf um den fruhen israelitischen Staat*. Neukirchen, Germany: Neukirchen Verlag.

Cullmann, O. (1950) *Christ and Time*. Philadelphia: The Westminster Press.

———— (1958) *The Immortality of the Soul or the Resurrection of the Body? The Witness of the New Testament*. London: Epworth Press.

Cunliffe-Jones, H. (1980) *A History of Christian Doctrine*. Philadelphia: Fortress Press.

Dawkins, R. (1998) *Unweaving the Rainbow: Science, Delusion and the Appetite for Wonder*. New York: Houghton Mifflin Co.

Deacon, T. W. (1997) *The Symbolic Species: The Co-Evolution of Language and the Brain*. New York: W. W. Norton.

Demski, W. A. and Behe, M. J. (1999) *Intelligent Design: The Bridge Between Science and Theology*. Downers Grove, Ill.: Intervarsity Press.

Driver, T. F. (1981) *Christ in a Changing World: Toward an Ethical Christology*. New York: Crossroad Publishing Company.

Durrant, M. (1973) *Theology and Intelligibility*. London: Routledge and Kegan Paul.

Duster, T. (1971) Conditions for Guilt-Free Massacre. In S. Nevitt and C. Comstock, eds. (pp. 25-36) *Sanctions for Evil: Sources of Social Destructiveness*. Boston, Mass.: Beacon Press.

Eastern Mennonite Board of Missions and Charities (1985) *Mennonite Witness as it Relates to Jewish People*. Salunga, Pa.: EMBMC.

Ehrenreich, B. (1997) *Blood Rites: Origins and History of the Passions of War*. New York: Henry Holt and Company.

Ellul, J. (1991) *Anarchy and Christianity*. Grand Rapids, Mich.: Wm. B. Eerdmans.

Eller, V. (1987) *Christian Anarchy*. Grand Rapids, Mich.: Wm. B. Eerdmans.

Etzioni, A. (1998) *The Essential Communitarian Reader*. Lanham, MD: Rowman and Littlefield.

Falk, M. (1989) Toward a Feminist Jewish Reconstruction of Monotheism. *TIKKUN*, July/August, 53-58.

Fingarette, H. (1996) *Death: Philosophical Soundings.* Chicago: Open Court.

Finger, T. N. (1989) *Christian Theology: An Eschatological Approach, Volume II.* Scottdale, Pa.: Herald Press.

Fischer, J. M. (1993) *The Metaphysics of Death.* Stanford, Calif.: Stanford University Press.

Fischer, R. M. S. (2001) The God Representation and the Inner Dialogue as Transitional Phenomena. In S. Aktar and H. Parens, eds. (pp. 53-74) *Does God Help? Developmental and Clinical Aspects of Religious Belief.* Northvale, N.J.: Jason Aronson, Inc.

Fischer, C. S. and Lasch, C. (1988) The Good Old Days. *TIKKUN,* Nov./Dec. 69-74.

Fleischner, E. (1977) *Auschwitz: Beginning of a New Era? Reflections on the Holocaust.* New York: KTAV

Fowler, J. W. (1981) *Stages of Faith: The Psychology of Human Development and the Quest for Meaning.* San Francisco, CA: Harper & Row.

Frankl, V. (1977) *Der unbewusste Gott: Psychotherapie und Religion.* Munich, Germany: Kosel Verlag.

Friesen, D. K. (1986) *Christian Peacemaking and International Conflict: A Realist Pacifist Perspective.* Scottdale, Pa.: Herald Press.

———— (2000) *Artists, Citizens, Philosophers: Seeking the Peace of the City.* Scottdale, Pa.: Herald Press.

Fromm, E. (1973) *The Anatomy of Human Destructiveness.* New York: Holt, Rinehart and Winston.

Gazzaniga, M. (1994) *Nature's Mind: The Biological Roots of Thinking, Emotions, Sexuality, Language and Intelligence.* New York: Basic Books

Girard, R. (1977) *Violence and the Sacred.* Baltimore: Johns Hopkins University Press.

———— (1986) *The Scapegoat.* Baltimore: Johns Hopkins University Press.

Gordis, D. (1995) *God Was Not In the Fire: The Search for a Spiritual Judaism.* New York: Scribners.

Gottwald, N. K. (1979) *The Tribes of Yahweh: A Sociology of the Religion of Liberated Israel 1250-1050 BCE.* Maryknoll, N.Y.: Orbis Books.

———— (1983) Sociological Method in the Study of Ancient Israel. In N.K. Gottwald, ed. (pp. 26-37) *The Bible and Liberation: Political and Social Hermeneutics.* Maryknoll, N.Y.: Orbis Books.

———— (1986) From Biblical Economies to Modern Economies. In W. K. Tabb, ed. (pp. 139-148) *Churches in Struggle: Liberation Theologies and Social Change in North America.* New York: Monthly Review Press.

Gramsci, A. (1957) *The Modern Prince and Other Writings* New York: International Publishers.

Grannis, C., Laffin, A. and Schade, E. (1981) *The Risk of the Cross: Christian Discipleship in the Nuclear Age.* New York: Seabury Press.

Greenberg, J., Solomon, S. and Pyszczynski, T. (1997) Terror Management Theory of Self-Esteem and Cultural Worldviews: Empirical Assessments and Conceptual Refinements. In M. P. Zanna, ed. *Advances in Experimental Social Psychology.* San Diego: Academic Press.

Grimsrud, T. (2000) *God's Healing Strategy*. Telford, Pa.: Pandora Press U.S.

Grossman, D. (1997) *On Killing: The Psychological Cost of Learning to Kill in War and Society*. Boston, Mass.: Little, Brown and Co.

—— and DeGaetano, G. (1999) *Stop Teaching Our Kids to Kill: A Call to Action Against TV, Movie & Video Game Violence*. New York: Crown Publishing.

Harnack, A. (1981) *Militia Christi: The Christian Religion and the Military in the First Three Centuries*. Philadelphia: Fortress Press.

Harrington, M. (1985) *The Politics at God's Funeral: The Spiritual Crisis of Western Civilization*. Harmondsworth, UK: Penguin Books.

Hengel, M. (1973) *Victory Over Violence: Jesus and the Revolutionaries*. Philadelphia: Fortress Press.

Hengel, M. (1974) *Property and Riches in the Early Church: Aspects of a Social History of Early Christianity*. Philadelphia: Fortress Press.

—— (1977) *Christ and Power*. Philadelphia: Fortress Press.

Hick, J. (1982) *God Has Many Names*. Philadelphia: Westminster Press.

—— (1989) *An Interpretation of Religion: Human Responses to the Transcendent*. New Haven, CT: Yale University Press.

—— (1995) *A Christian Theology of Religions: The Rainbow of Faiths*. Louisville, Ky.: Westminster John Knox Press.

—— and Hebblethwaite, B. (1980) *Christianity and Other Religions*. Philadelphia: Fortress Press.

Hocking, W. E. (1957) *The Meaning of Immortality in Human Experience*. New York: Harper Brothers.

Hornus, J. M. (1980) *It Is Not Lawful for Me to Fight: Early Christian Attitudes Toward War, Violence and the State*. Scottdale, Pa.: Herald Press.

Holzner, B. (1967) *Reality Construction in Society*. Cambridge, Mass.: Schenkman Publishing Company.

Horsley, R. (1993) *Jesus and the Spiral of Violence: Popular Jewish Resistance in Roman Palestine*. Minneapolis, Minn.: Fortress Press.

Jacobs, L. (1988) *Principles of the Jewish Faith*. Northvale, N.J.: Jason Aronson, Inc.

Kamenetz. R. (1994) *The Jew and the Lotus: A Poet's Rediscovery of Jewish Identity in Buddhist India*. San Francisco, CA: Harper Collins.

Kass, L. R. (2001) Preventing a Brave New World: Why We Should Ban Human Cloning Now. *The New Republic*, 224 (21), 31-39.

Katz, S. T. (1983) *Post-Holocaust Dialogues: Critical Studies in Modem Jewish Thought*. New York: NYU Press.

Kauffman, J. (1995) *Awareness of Mortality*. Amityville, N.Y.: Baywood Publishing Company.

Kaufman, G. D. (1972) *God: The Problem*. Cambridge, Mass.: Harvard University Press.

—— (1975) *An Essay in Theological Method*. Missoula, Mont.: Scholars Press.

—— (1981) *The Theological Imagination: Constructing the Concept of God*. Philadelphia: Westminster Press.

—— (1985a) *Theology for a Nuclear Age*. Philadelphia: Westminster Press.

—— Kaufman, G. D. (1985b) The Nature of Doctrine. (Review). *Theology Today, 42,* 240-241

—— Kaufman, G. D. (1993) *In Face of Mystery: A Constructive Theology*. Cambridge, Mass.: Harvard University Press.

—— Kaufman, G. D. (1995). *God, Mystery, Diversity*. Minneapolis, Minn.: Augsburg Fortress Press.

Keen, S. (1974) A Day of Loving Combat: Interview with Ernest Becker. *Psychology Today,* (April) 71-80.

—— (1986) *Faces of the Enemy*. New York: Harper & Row.

Kegan, R. (1983) *The Evolving Self*. Cambridge, Mass.: Harvard University Press.

Kierkegaard, S. (1983) *Sickness Unto Death*. Princeton, N.J.: Princeton University Press.

Knitter, P. (1985) *No Other Name? A Critical Survey Christian Attitudes Toward the World Religions*. Maryknoll, N.Y.: Orbis Books.

Kohlberg, L. (1981) *The Meaning and Measurement of Moral Development*. Worcester, MA: Clark University Heinz Werner Institute.

Kung, H. (1976) *On Being a Christian*. New York: Doubleday.

—— (1988) *Theology for the Third Millennium: An Ecumenical View*. New York: Doubleday.

—— and Tracy, D. (1984) *Theologie-Wohin? Auf dem Weg zu einem neuen Paradigma*. Gutersloh, Germany: Gutersloher Verlagshaus Gerd Mohn.

—— (1986) *Das neue Paradigma von Theologie: Strukturen und Dimensionen* Gutersloh, Germany: Gutersloher Verlagshaus Gerd Mohn.

Lakoff, G. and Johnson, M. (1999) *Philosophy in the Flesh: The Embodied Mind and Its Challenge to Western Thought*. New York: Basic Books.

Langer, S. K. (1957) *Philosophy in a New Key*. Cambridge, Mass.: Harvard University Press.

Lanternari, V. (1965) *The Religions of the Oppressed: A Study of Modern Messianic Cults*. New York: American Library.

Lapide, P. (1980) *Er predigte in ihren Synagogen: Judische Evangelienauslegung*. Gutersloh, Germany: Gutersloher Verlagshaus Gerd Mohn.

Lasch, C. (1989) Progress: The Last Superstition. *TIKKUN,* May/June, 27-33.

Lerner, M. (1994) *Jewish Renewal: A Path to Healing and Transformation*. New York: Grosset/Putnam.

Liechty, D. (1984) Free Church Assumptions in a Christian Approach to Marxism. *Conrad Grebel Review, 2,* 211-217.

—— (1986) Christian Freedom and Political Freedom. *Conrad Grebel Review, 4,* 101-23.

—— (1990) *Theology in Postliberal Perspective*. Philadelphia: Trinity Press International.

—— (1994) *Early Anabaptist Spirituality: Selected Writings*. Mahwah, N.J.: Paulist Press.

—— (1995). *Transference and Transcendence: Ernest Becker's Contribution to Psychotherapy.* Northvale, N.J.: Jason Aronson, Inc.

—— (1996) The Seamless Robe of Human Experience: An Essay on (Mennonite) Theological Method. In A. E. Weaver, ed. (pp. 80-91) *Mennonite Theology in Face of Modernity: Essays in Honor of Gordon D. Kaufman.* North Newton, Kan. Bethel Press.

—— (1998a) Reaction to Mortality: An Interdisciplinary Organizing Principle for the Human Sciences. *Zygon: The Journal of Science and Religion, 33,* 45-59.

—— (1998b) Reading Ernest Becker: His Contribution to Spiritual, Pastoral and Psychological Counseling. *American Journal of Pastoral Counseling, 1,* 49-69

—— (1999a) The *Denial of Death* revisited. *Death Studies, 4(8),* 757-760.

—— (1999b) What Kind of Political Power? In T. Grimsrud and L. Johns, eds. (pp. 17-33) *Peace and Justice Shall Embrace: Power and Theopolitics in the Bible.* Telford, Pa.: Pandora Press U.S.

—— (2000) Communication Technology and the Development of Consciousness: Reframing the Discussion of Anabaptists and Postmodernity. *Conrad Grebel Review, 18,* 28-47.

—— (2003) *Death and Denial: Interdisciplinary Essays on the Legacy of Ernest Becker.* Westport, Conn.: Praeger Publishing Company.

Lifton, R. J. and Markusen, E. (1990) *Genocidal Mentality: Nazi Holocaust and Nuclear Threat.* New York: Basic Books.

—— (1979) *The Broken Connection: On Death and the Continuity of Life.* New York: Simon and Schuster.

Lind, M. C. (1980) *Yahweh Is a Warrior: The Theology of Warfare in Ancient Israel.* Scottdale, Pa.: Herald Press.

—— (1990) *Monotheism, Power, Justice.* Elkhart, Ind.: Institute of Mennonite Studies.

Lindbeck, G. (1984) *The Nature of Doctrine: Religion and Theology in a Postliberal Age.* Louisville, Ky.: Westminster John Knox Press.

Loy, D. (1996) *Lack and Transcendence: The Problem of Death and Life in Psychotherapy, Existentialism and Buddhism.* Atlantic Heights, N.J.: Humanities Press.

MacQuarrie, J. (1963) *Twentieth Century Religious Thought.* London: SCM Press.

Martin, D. (1978) *A General Theory of Secularization.* New York: Harper & Row.

Marxsen, W. (ND) *Die Sache Jesu geht weiter* Gutersloh, Germany: Gutersloher Verlagshaus Gerd Mohn.

McGiffert, C. (1932) *A History of Christian Thought: Early and Eastern.* New York: Scribners.

McCoy, C. S. (1980) *When Gods Change: Hope For Theology.* Nashville, Tenn.: Abingdon Press.

McFague, S. (1987) *Models of God: Theology for an Ecological, Nuclear Age.* Philadelphia: Fortress Press.

Min, A. K. (1989) How Not to Do a Theology of Liberation: A Critique of Schubert Ogden. *Journal of the American Academy of Religion, 57,* 83-102.

Mouw, R. J. (1994) *Consulting the Faithful: What Christian Intellectuals Can Learn From Popular Religion.* Grand Rapids, Mich.: Wm. B. Eerdmans.

Munz, P. (1964) *Relationship and Solitude: A Study of the Relationship Between Ethics, Metaphysics and Mythology.* London: Eyre and Spottiswoode.

Nelson, J. R. (1994) *On the New Frontiers of Genetics and Religion.* Grand Rapids, Mich.: Wm. B. Eerdmans.

Nelson-Pallmeyer, J. (2001) *Jesus Against Christianity: Reclaiming the Missing Jesus.* Harrisburg, Pa.: Trinity Press International.

Neusner, J. (1993) *A Rabbi Talks With Jesus: An Intermillennial, Interfaith Exchange.* New York: Doubleday.

Newberg, A. and D'Aquili, E. (2001) *Why God Won't Go Away: Brain Science and the Biology of Belief.* New York: Ballantine Books.

Niebuhr, R. (1941) *The Nature and Destiny of Man. Volume One: Human Nature.* New York: Scribners.

Nietzsche, F. (1966) *Beyond Good and Evil.* New York: Vintage Books.

Nigg, W. (1949) *Das Buch der Ketzer.* Zurich: Artemis Verlag.

Nyce, D. Y. (2000) Disciplined Interreligious Dialogue. *Anabaptist-Mennonite Scholars Network, 3(2),* 1-3.

Pagels, E. (1979) *The Gnostic Gospels.* New York: Random House.

—— (1988) *Adam, Eve, and the Serpent.* New York: Random House.

Perrin, N. (1963) *The Kingdom of God in the Teaching of Jesus.* Philadelphia: The Westminster Press.

—— (1967) *Rediscovering the Teaching of Jesus.* New York: Harper & Row.

Perrin, N. (1968) The Son of man in the Synoptic Tradition. *Biblical Research, 13,* 1-23

Phillips, J. B. (1952) *Your God Is Too Small.* New York: Macmillan.

Pohier, J. (1977) *Quand je dis Dieu.* Paris, FR: Editions du Seuil.

—— (1985) *God: In Fragments.* New York: Crossroad Publishing Company.

Rahner, K. (1965ff) *Theological Investigations, Volumes 12 and 14.* New York: Seabury Press.

Rapoport, A. (1954) *Operational Philosophy: Integrating Knowledge and Action.* New York: Harper Brothers.

Rank, O. (1971) *The Double: A Psychoanalytic Study.* Chapel Hill, N.C.: University of North Carolina Press.

Rantala, M. L. and Milgram, A. J. eds. (1999) *Cloning: For and Against.* Chicago: Open Court.

Reich, W. (1971) *The Mass Psychology of Fascism.* New York: Farrar, Straus, Giroux.

Reimer, A. J. (2001) *Mennonites and Classical Theology: Dogmatic Foundations for Christian Ethics.* Kitchener, Ont.: Pandora Press.

Ricoeur, P. (1969) *The Symbolism of Evil.* Boston, Mass.: Beacon Press.

Rizzuto, A. M. (2001) Does God Help? What God? Helping Whom? The Convolutions of Divine Help. In S. Aktar and H. Parens, eds. (pp. 19-52). *Does God Help? Developmental and Clinical Aspects of Religious Belief.* Northvale, N.J.: Jason Aronson, Inc.

Rolheiser, R. (1999) *The Holy Longing: The Search for A Christian Spirituality*. New York: Doubleday.

de Rougemont, D. (1941) On the Devil and Politics, *Christianity and Crisis*, June 1941, reprinted in W. H. Cowan, ed. (1966) *Witness to a Generation* (pp. 6-12). Indianapolis, Ind.: Bobbs-Merrill Co.

Russell, J. (1977) *The Devil: Perceptions of Evil from Antiquity to Primitive Christianity*. Ithaca, N.Y.: Cornell University Press.

————— (1981) *Satan: The Early Christian Tradition*. Ithaca, N.Y.: Cornell University Press.

————— (1984) *Lucifer: The Devil in the Middle Ages*. Ithaca, N.Y.: Cornell University Press.

————— (1988) *The Prince of Darkness: Radical Evil and the Power of Good in History*. Ithaca, N.Y.: Cornell University Press.

St. John of the Cross (1959) *Dark Night of the Soul*. New York: Image Books.

Sartre, J. P. (1968) *Being and Nothingness*. New York: Citadel Press.

Schillebeeckx, E. (1979) *Jesus: An Experiment in Christology*. New York: Seabury Press.

Schmidt, F. W. (2000) *The Changing Face of God*. Harrisburg, Pa.: Morehouse Publishing.

Schrottroff, W. and Stegemann, W. (1984) *God of the Lowly: Socio-Historical Interpretations of the Bible*. Maryknoll, N.Y.: Orbis Books.

Schultz, H. J. (1968) *Die Wahrheit der Ketzer*. Stuttgart, Germany: Kreuz Verlag.

Schwager, R. (1987) *Must There Be Scapegoats? Violence and Redemption in the Bible*. San Francisco: Harper & Row.

Segal, A.F. (1999) Two Powers in Heaven and Early Christian Trinitarian Thinking. In S.T. Davis, D. Kendall and G. O'Collins, eds. (73-95) *The Trinity: An Interdisciplinary Symposium on the Trinity*. New York: Oxford University Press.

Segundo, J. L. (1988) *An Evolutionary Approach to Jesus of Nazareth*. Maryknoll, N.Y.: Orbis Books.

Sheehan, T. (1986) *The First Coming: How the Kingdom of God Became Christianity*. New York: Random House.

Shenk, D. W. (1995) *Global Gods: Exploring the Role of Religions in Modern Society*. Scottdale, Pa.: Herald Press.

Shenk, D. W. (1997) *A Muslim and a Christian In Dialogue*. Scottdale, Pa.: Herald Press.

Solomon, S., Greenberg, J., and Pyszczynski, T. (1991) A Terror Management Theory of Social Behavior: The Psychological Functions of Self-Esteem and Cultural Worldviews. In M. P. Zanna, ed. *Advances in Experimental Social Psychology*. San Diego: Academic Press.

————— and Pyszczynski, T. (1998) Tales From the Crypt: On the Role of Death In Life. *Zygon: The Journal of Science and Religion, 33*, 9-44.

Staub, E. (1989) *The Roots of Evil: The Origins of Genocide and Other Group Violence*. New York: Cambridge University Press.

Streng, F. J., Lloyd, C. L. and Allen, J. T. (1973) *Ways of Being Religious: Readings for a New Approach to Religion.* Englewood Cliffs, N.J.: Prentice-Hall, Inc.

Stutzman, L. and Shenk, D.W. eds. (1999) *Practicing Truth: Confident Witness In Our Pluralistic World.* Scottdale, Pa.: Herald Press.

Swartley, W., ed. (2000) *Violence Renounced: Rene Girard, Biblical Studies and Peacemaking.* Telford, Pa.: Pandora Press U.S.

Vahanian, G. (1966) *No Other God.* New York: George Braziller.

Voegelin, E. (1966) *The New Science of Politics.* Chicago: University of Chicago Press.

Walsh, J. P. M. (1987) *The Mighty from Their Thrones: Power in the Biblical Tradition.* Philadelphia: Fortress Press.

Walzer, M. (1985) *Exodus and Revolution.* New York: Basic Books.

Weaver, J. D. (2000) *Anabaptist Theology in the Face of Postmodernity: A Proposal for the Third Millennium.* Telford, Pa.: Pandora Press U.S.

Weigert, A. J. (1988) Christian Eschatological Identities in the Nuclear Context. *Journal for the Scientific Study of Religion,* 27 (2), 175-91.

Westphal, M. (1987) *God, Guilt and Death.* Bloomington, Ind.: Indiana University Press.

Williams, J. G. (1991) *The Bible, Violence and the Sacred: Liberation From the Myth of Sanctioned Violence.* San Francisco: HarperCollins.

Wink, W. (1984). *Naming the Powers: The Language of Power in the New Testament.* Philadelphia: Fortress Press

——— (1986) *Unmasking the Powers: The Invisible Forces that Determine Human Existence.* Philadelphia: Fortress Press.

——— (1992) *Engaging the Powers: Discernment and Resistance in a World of Domination.* Minneapolis, Minn.: Fortress Press.

——— (1998) *The Powers That Be: Theology for a New Millennium.* New York: Doubleday.

Wright, R. (1995) *The Moral Animal: Why We Are the Way We Are.* New York: Vintage Books.

Yoder, J. H. (1972) *The Politics of Jesus: Vicit Angus Noster.* Grand Rapids, Mich.: Wm. B. Eerdmans.

——— (1984) *The Priestly Kingdom: Social Ethics as Gospel.* Notre Dame, Ind.: University of Notre Dame Press.

THE INDEX

THE AUTHOR

*D*aniel Liechty was raised in Berne, Indiana and is a graduate of Eastern Mennonite High School, of Eastern Mennonite College, and of Mennonite Biblical Seminary. After spending three years on assignment in Europe with the Mennonite Central Committee, Liechty completed doctoral studies at the University of Vienna in Austria. His research focused on Sabbatarian ideology among Anabaptists and Unitarians in East Central Europe. Upon returning to the United States, Liechty became interested in mental health issues and completed graduate degrees in clinical social work and pastoral counseling.

He served several years at the Institute of Pennsylvania Hospital in Philadelphia, where he specialized in group work. During this time he developed an increasing interest in issues of grief, death and dying, and subsequently moved into a clinical social work practice at the Montgomery (Pa.) Medical Center Hospice Program, where he also served as a member of the hospital ethics committee. In 1999, he joined the Graduate Faculty of Illinois State University (Normal, Ill.) in the School of Social Work.

Liechty has published many books, chapters, and articles related to history, religion and mental health, and clinical social work practice. A member of Germantown Mennonite Church in Philadelphia, he attends services at Mennonite Church of Normal as well as at Moses Montefiore Synagogue of Normal. He is married to Naomi Wilansky, a clinical social worker, and they have a young daughter, Hannah Miriam.

A lover of roots music, Liechty has performed in acoustic bluegrass, country, and blues groups. He now performs with the Reunion Vocal Band (folk/country) and Bloomsday (Celtic), is a musician for The Dances of Universal Peace, and takes part in an emerging Yiddish/Klezmer singing ensemble in Normal.